The Awakening of a
WARRIOR-ANGEL

MECKRON SERAPH

BALBOA.
PRESS
A DIVISION OF HAY HOUSE

Balboa Press books may be ordered through booksellers or by contacting:

Balboa Press
A Division of Hay House
1663 Liberty Drive
Bloomington, IN 47403
www.balboapress.com
1-(877) 407-4847

ISBN: 978-1-4525-3902-7 (sc)
ISBN: 978-1-4525-3903-4 (e)

Because of the dynamic nature of the Internet, any web addresses or
links contained in this book may have changed since publication and
may no longer be valid. The views expressed in this work are solely those
of the author and do not necessarily reflect the views of the publisher,
and the publisher hereby disclaims any responsibility for them.

The author of this book does not dispense medical advice or prescribe the use
of any technique as a form of treatment for physical, emotional, or medical
problems without the advice of a physician, either directly or indirectly. The
intent of the author is only to offer information of a general nature to help
you in your quest for emotional and spiritual well-being. In the event you use
any of the information in this book for yourself, which is your constitutional
right, the author and the publisher assume no responsibility for your actions.

Any people depicted in stock imagery provided by Thinkstock are models,
and such images are being used for illustrative purposes only.

Certain stock imagery © Thinkstock.

Printed in the United States of America

Balboa Press rev. date: 09/27/2011

Contents

"Dedicated to my wife."

ACKNOWLEDGEMENTS:

First, I wish to thank my guardian angel, Kathy, for helping me on the right path.

Also, I would like to thank my wonderful family, who helped me to become what I am today and for your loving support.

I`d like to thank mr. Michael Ebeling at the Ebeling & Associates Literary Agency, Mollie Harrison, Mara Rockey, Jennifer Slaybaugh and the Balboa Press team for your wonderful help.

And the most and the warmest of all—I want to thank you, my dear Samia. My Eternal Wife. For your Love.

Thank you!

FOREWORD:

Have you ever though about why we are here?
Or who we are?
Or are we just some unsignificant dots in the Allness, living our lives unnoticably?
Or does it matter at all what we do in life, when there is no-one to witness it?
Does anyone care of our billions of choices in life, that seemingly are swallowed by the hungry mouth of the deep Sea of Apathy?
Well, I hadn`t. But if I had, I would of been elected to be the mayor of the Ignoranceville, for what was waiting for me . . .

CHAPTER ONE
"RISING TO THE SURFACE"

"It's not the Darkness, that puts out the Light in the evening—it is the Light that puts out the Darkness in the morning."

—*an unknown author*

THE TOUCH OF AN ANGEL

On that morning I woke up as usual.

The Moon rolled her rays through the window. It was a dark winter. I liked the winter—it reminded me of peace.

I was just like anyone else. A 14-year-old school-kid. I believe the word that I am looking for, is "normal".

My school-road mirrored all my 8 years in school. This road was the best part of my day—it made me feel that I am who I am and I don't have to be more.

The bluish-silver sky, resting on the top of the frosted trees. But me . . . I'm going to somewhere—where? I feel like I'm apart from everything—why?

The school—this was the place where I learned that I do not know anything. I learned how I am nobody and that I do not know where I'm headed, and in particular—how not to know what I was doing.

Our Russian teacher was teaching impeccably the grammar rules of the foreign language, but I couldn't understand what it had to do with anything? With my life, I mean. With the gasp that I felt inside me, I was looking at the only supportive freind I had—it's yellow worn corners. I liked that desk.

I was peering, emotionless, on the words scribbled on that desk by someone, when I suddenly heared:

"Meckron, why are you here?"

I raised my smaller-sunken sleepy eyes.

The teacher was still speaking, the classmates were trying to follow her as they could.

But there it was again:

"Meckron . . . Who are you? Why are you here?"

"What is this?" I thought to myself. "What was I thinking? Did I read it somewhere? No. But how was my thought addressing to me?"

I focused on the question in my thoughts, when suddenly I heard it again:

"Who are you and why are you here?"

Though it seemed ridiculous, I decided to respond to my thought with the thought:

"I'm at school, because I have to."

I felt lighter somehow. Perhaps because I expressed my feelings, defining my place in life.

"I'd like to be your deskmate," the *thought* in my head became more vivid and distinctive: "Then you could see me every day."

"What is wrong with me?" I was thinking, without addressing to my *thought-friend*.

But the thought answered:

"You just don`t know why you're here, that`s all."

I focused on the teacher. I didn`t know what to think of all this. But I felt better. Something was more calm and clearer inside me.

On the evening, as I was making a snowy traces as heading home, I wasn`t the same.

Where was I or what was I doing all day?

I couldn`t actually recollect it all. For some reason, it haunted me, that I wasn`t able to give the meaning to my schoolday. It didn`t make any sense to me, like it did before. Sure, I was there for learning. But what was I learning for? Did I learn to change, like I did today? Something changed, that`s for sure.

"What difference does it make?" I thought to myself.

That was my all-defining answer to everything on that time. The only thing that emerged from my well-done day, was a special surprising *thought* in my head.

"Right . . ." I mumbled, walking through the snowdrifts: "I`ve probably seen too many movies, I suppose."

It was not an exaggeration, I tell you that.

"Hey, deskmate! You didn`t do a fig for yourself today."

I winced and my stomach shrank in seizures. This *thought* came to me from my left, outside of me this time.

It was not even the *thought*, more like the dream voice—a kind of a voice like the characters in our dreams have at night.

It would have seemed cosmically ridiculous claim if I had said it, because I was the boy who jumped on the walls and drilled his words into every conversation on horizon.

"I ate today," I objected.

"It was not really for you, if it has no meaning for you. Besides—you did it wrong," the *thought* claimed happily.

I shook my head, watching the snow falling from the trees:

"My own *thought* gives me a hard time."

"Why do you think that I am your thought?" I heard as soon as I got over with that sentence.

"And what are you then?"

"I'm like you. And I want to help you. You know who I am. But you won`t get better grades in school for this wisdom" the *dream-voice* responded supportively.

"I didn't count on it," I replied, thinking that I have a nose-wise angel . . .

It was like a flash through my consciousness. I heard something cracked in the depths of my mind.

That word! There was a recognition in me or something like that.

"Are you . . . ?" My eyes were probably already size of a cabbages.

"An angel," was the answer and she started laughing: "Well done, 10 points!"

I was standing and looking at one spot, with nothing in my mind for a long time. My internal dialog was silenced.

It seemed that I was away somewhere. All the way, there was only silence, endless peace and quietness.

If I was myself again, I tried to focus the location of the *voice*. It was on my right this time.

"If you need me, just call me, think of me," I heard clearly.

"Do you have a name?" I asked, in the comprehensive embrace of amaze.

"Kathiania" was the answer.

I got home and my old perception recovered. I submerged in my usual doings, until evening, when my shallow mind-noise was silenced.

In a warm bed, under a blue blanket, I thought about my day.

"What if I do not have the meaning of what I was doing today?" was the most haunting question in me.

I decided to try:

"Kathiania!" I called her.

Before I called her, I felt her beside me.

"You're like a creepy phantom dream," I said to her, knowing that she is present.

"And You are like a man in a TV-show," I heard a laugh.

Great. I have a sarcastic guardian angel.

"Are you always like this?" I asked, thinking that angels should speak differently.

"I use your language, my dear. You can also master all the languages, you just have to embrace them," she replied cheerfully.

This was the time when I didn't understand a lot what she was saying.

I asked further:

"What do you mean: I didn't do anything for myself today?"

"To do something for yourself—is to do something for everyone," was a warmly kind answer.

"What do you mean?"

"If you're doing something, it is reflected from the Light, and returns to you in multiplicity. What did you do today, that you would want to get back in multiplicity?" her voice sounded pretty compassionate.

Nothing came to mind.

"Yes, you ate," she said. "And now people will return this favor to you, by eating in full multiplicity."

I laughed out loud in my soft bed.

I was tired, so I fell asleep and I don't even know exactly when I entered into the dreamland.

THE NEW DAWN

As I woke up in the morning, I rushed hazily to school.

Something had changed. I felt the anticipation for the oncoming day.

"Why?" I was thinking. "A normal school day was ahead."

But this was anything else but normal. Something in that fresh day actually meant something to me. And I didn`t know what.

The feathery snowflakes fell on my shoulders without a sound. All was quiet. Quiet as the anticipation in me. It was like a sound or the feeling of felling in love.

I reached for the high brown school-door, that was located to the south of the building and the sun had warmed it in the morning.

I opened the door and let another student in, before I entered. It was something, that I had not previously done so, living in the little box, labeled "selfishness".

"That *is* the meaning of it all!" I thought, entering the sunny doors.

"I'm at school, to do good. To help others."

My mind suddenly was filled with a high ringlike tone, like a crystal. I never felt the anticipation for the on-coming day. Now I felt it for nothing and for everything.

"Here's the truth," Kathiania was by my side when I swapped shoes, in dressing room.

"We live in a world of Invisibility—in the world of the warrior-angels—you and me. We're here to help people. To do good. And to inspire everyone around you to do it."

"Why?" I asked, ignoring the unbelievability of the conversation at hand.

"Because the seed is an invisible tree."

"I don't understand," I whispered, and one of my classmates looked at me as if my shoe-knot was unsolvable mystery to me.

"It means," the guardian angel went on, "that the reality of a warrior-angel lies in his feelings, meanings and doings. It is a world as visible or unvisible like every other."

She spoke with a voice, similar to a thought.

I felt how right she was. The reflections, shadows and the illusions of egoistic needs and fears of a "real world", went by me and did not mean anything to me. I didn't *feel* the achievements in my life or the anticipation or inspiration to do anything what I was doing daily. Thousands of random things that filled my life. I didn't even remember most of them. How did I become to be so cut off?

For my sorrow, I discovered that this law also governs the people around me. They weren't real, I didn't felt them in my life. At least not as real as Kathiania was becoming for me.

I was truly living in the invisible walls of the social Alcatraz and I didn't know who holds the key.

At some point of the day, I could not longer tolerate the emptiness of my life and the lack of love, which was later revealed, that had also been an illusion of mine. A lot of teenagers have that.

Probably I craved for something warm, because I asked from my guardian angel:

"Kathy!" I called her by the nickname. "If you're an angel, then you know all kinds of stuff, right?"

"I also know the stuff, that stuff don`t know about," I heard a high voice tone, or laughter.

"Then you also know whether some girl in this school loves me.?"

"Meckron, what is that question for?" was the answer.

"No reason . . ."

I thought that this is something to know after all. To get the answer to my question was, of course, an immature hope:

"Do you not feel it yourself?" was a straight response.

"What do you mean? Of course not. Surely, I am not a mind-reader."

"But if you don`t feel the heat of her love, then what do you need to know it for?"

In the beginning, Kathy seemed irritating to me with her not-responding sparring.

She continued:

"Even if someone loves you, the girls I mean, then it wouldn`t be anything to do with you."

"I beg your pardon?" I knew how to make myself extremely stupid. I learned that from school.

"Let's say that someone loves you," she continued, "have you ever given something to her?"

"What?"

I didn`t even know who she was talking about.

"Have you done something good for her, Meckron?"

"I don`t know."

"Have you done something for anyone, to make someone to love you?"

I shook my head, starting to realize, where Kathy was aiming that snowball:

"The other people's feelings doesn't depend on me, do they?"

"No. They do not."

I leaned against a window table on the corridor.

Kathy went on:

"When someone loves you, it's because she is happy to do so. Because she wants to be feeling so. It is unconditional love. But if you learn about the other person's warmth of love, to percieve its source, to comprehend it, then someday you can help someone to love."

"Help someone to love? How?"

"To help her to be able to love. For unconditional love."

"Able to love?" in school I was taught to ask questions. That's a plus.

"Love is like a plant," Kathy continued, "she lives and grows where conditions are favorable. To create the conditions, one can be helped. As long as your ego wants to know if someone is captured by you, charmed by you, you can not feel the source of love."

"I see . . ."

I thought that I understood. If that would have been so, many days would've seen more sun in my future.

"So one can feel it, if one is loved?" I asked further.

"Of course! After all, that is what love is all about—if you feel the warmth of love of someone, you can multiply it, by mirroring it back to her, in the lightfulness of inspiration. Love is what makes the eternity possible. But first, it is necessary to learn about love—just like you need to learn about the plant, if you are starting to build your garden."

I looked how the children of the first grade, whirled pass by me like a snowstorm

Suddenly, it felt like a warm lamp shined on me and it came from somewhere on my right and moved around me.

"Finally!" Kathy joked. "A big star has arrived to our gala! All the spotlights are pointed on him! Fans gone crazy ! . . ."

Kathy went on joking, but I, for the first time, *felt* her! Not her words or thoughts, or how real she was, but the warmth that she was emitting. A something like a heat.

Was that the warmth of love?

I did not ask her. I heared the schoolbell, and I went to the classroom and cheerfully, someone opened the door for me and let me in first.

Kathy had been right again.

THE DIVINE WILL

The following days were increasingly wonderful. I discovered that I`m feeling. Sharper. I wasn`t previously noticed my feelings so clearly, or at least I wasn`t aware of it.

I did not do particularly good to anyone, but I had hope to do it. At least I had a reason to wake up in the morning, and this reason was my own . . . really my own decision—a choice. It made me stronger and clearer.

On one evening, my warm guardian angel appeared:

"Hey, how are you?" she asked warmly and always with a genuine interest and love.

"Fine. And you?"

"Oh, very wonderfully. No-one has asked me this for a long time," Kathy laughed.

I was starting to perceive her more clearly every day. It seemed to me, that she was like a young girl, but I could not see her details. It seemed, like she was a warmness that had a shape. A loom shape. But I heard her more clearly now.

"The tomorrow depends on you, do you know that?"

She said it, squatting next to my bed.

"You want to say that I can make it better, right? But it is very difficult for me to find people whom to help. It`s like there is no such people, or . . ."

I plundged into thoughts. Kathy never interrupted, when I was thinking.

When I came back into that moment, she replied:

""The next day does not only depend on your actions. And not only on your achievements. As you walk on Earth, you have a supreme power: to *will* what the day would be tomorrow. All the visible and invisible in the Allness, is bowed to that *will*."

Kathy used the words in shapes that were known to me. Now I know that this phenomenon is called *the will of intent*.

I laughed:

"I have wanted a lot of things. Why, then, the world is not like I *willed*?"

"You're doing it wrong!"

It seemed to me that she was imitating a teacher from my chemistry class. We both laughed.

"I will teach you. It will open for you over the years. The *will*—it is the Law. Everything listens to that Law. It is a God's gift to you at birth. If you *will* from God, it shall be so."

It took me a several years to understand how easy and difficult was to understand this sentence.

"Mh?" I frowned. I hadn`t thought a lot about the spiritual laws on that time.

"But, Kathy, how do one *wills* then?"

It seemed to me that the angel nodded, and started from scratch:

"It is important that you know *who you are*. For example, if you know that you're a school kid, then tomorrow or a week or a year to come, it has something to do with the school. In this case, it is about what a school kid wants and the world offers him that. Although it is important to choose what you wish, the *will* does not come from one`s thoughts."

"Where does it come from?"

"The *will,* which creates the tomorrow, comes from the deeper "I". This conviction comes from who we are. From whom we feel ourselves to be. Your superficial desires didn`t come into the World, because you didn`t really believe that it was you, who wanted it."

I tried to think about what she said, as she continued:

"But now, imagine that you are a warrior-angel. You are the Savior of the World. Tomorrow's world depends on you. You recieved this purpose from the Powers that Be. All that you *intent,* will come true. Just like it came to be what the God *willed.* You do remember Him—your Dad, don`t you?"

Suddenly I felt a jolt and something inside of me went to it`s place. I do not know what it was. It reminded me a recognition of something so dear, but I also had the sensation of being scattered throughout the world, melted to it`s particles.

I couldn`t say a word anymore.

I only remember one point, in that great overflow of pure feelings:

"If I'm the world's savior, then I would need to know how everything is around me, and beyond. Is everything okay with the other people. Does anyone needs my help . . . I *will . . .*"

The next thing I remember, was a stormy sea, which was beating against the high walls of a stone coast. It was not in Estonia. I felt like I was in a dream, only that I was awake! Was I there with my body?!

I just flew like a plane around the storm at night, along the shore, studying the waves and the banks and the stones.

Suddenly I was back in my bed and I could feel Kathy at my side.

"WOW! That was cool, I was like in a dream, only I wasn`t asleep! Kathy!"

"You *willed* to . . ." she replied. "This is one of your abilities. A human being`s abilities. And a warrior-angel should be aware of this ability to use it for the good of Mankind."

The next school days whizzed by me like the postmen. I only remember the conversations with Kathy.

I was like living in two different worlds, I began to feel like I did not belong in eighter one. I felt as I was becoming a two different people.

I could not share my reality with my friends or anyone, because I did not know exactly how to describe it. What could I say? That I was dreaming awake? That I speak with someone who resembles a character in a dream? An imaginary chick, called Kathy?

No, thank you. I`ll better be nobody.

"The feeling of distance," Kathy explained, "is because you're starting to live outside the body. It is necessary to understand the *will*."

My guardian angel was the only point of sanity for me on that time. Though I was still not thoroughly convinced of her existence, I could not allowed myself to believe otherwise, because her words kept me in one piece. In one person.

She only joked about it, like always:

"I'm like a chair, that you chose. Soon you will understand the floor."

On one evening, Kathy came to me again, but her voice was more accurate and more specific:

"You need to go to sleep now. Your help is required."

"Where?" I asked myself, noticing that I can almost see the shady outline of her.

"In another world."

"I'm going into another world? Why?"

"Only if you want to help," Kathy said and continued, "you're a warrior-angel who has never been defeated. Many of them do not even try. That's why They were willing to send you."

"Who?"

"The Higher Powers."

"What is wrong and where?"

"Just go to sleep, dear Meckron, there you have it easier to understand, I'll explain it to you there."

I did not know just what to expect. I went to bed, willing to help.

I woke up in the night-wind, which mysteriously rustled in the dark alder branches.

"I'm not in my bed!" I thought, but my thoughts were so loud as words. I remembered what Kathy had told me. As soon as I remembered it, I heard her voice, not by my side, but from the distance.

She sounded like a telephone:

"You have to stop him. Only, if you meet acquaintances there, do not let them to understand that you're not the Meckron of their world. And do not let that other Meckron see you."

"Ok!"

Somehow what she said was very logical, as I had known it already. I had also a huge self-confidence and knowing what needs to be done.

It was dark and I knew that I had to go to the direction, following my senses.

I reached to the green trees, behind them was a building. All very similar to "my world", only that everyone was a little slower—like in a slow motion.

In that place I had the will, because I knew who I was. I certainly wasn`t the self-centered 14-year-old school boy.

I was a warrior-angel.

Suddenly, from hights, a man descended near me, entirely in black and a little surprised to see me. The anger rose in him and he came towards me with a roar and shot a fireball from his hand.

I dodged it with a firm move to the right and he immediately sent a new ball of fire towards me.

I raised my left hand and stopped it—it was my will. And suddenly I knew that I can move with a tremendous speed. With a glimpse, I was behind him and pushed him down. Somehow, he bursted into flames, as I pushed him into the ground. Only the extinguishing sparks flew around me in silence, and I woke into my bed. It was the morning.

"Nice!" Kathy laughed beside me and clapping. I discovered that I perceive her appearance. She had long straight black hair and blue eyes, a young woman she was.

"Was it real?" I asked her.

"No more real than the fact that you are in this bed," she shook her head seriously, and then cast out a laugh.

"Why didn`t I see you there?"

"I kept the distance," Kathy said with a voice and the language of a young child and continued, "I have the helping-vow."

"We`ll talk later," I said and put my school clothes on—it`s not just the fireballs there, that you have to worry about.

WHO ARE YOU, KATHY?

I could feel the world differently. I noticed that I have difficulty in bringing myself out from the fascination, as I glanced the floating treetops in peering winds, thick clouds, or the setting sun`s flaming and an ancient fir forest greenery.

There was something living in me, and that something was trying to tell me, that I am loved infinitely.

I asked about it from my beloved guardian angel:

"Do you look and feel like that as well, Kathy?"

"No, my dear. The communication with Dad is different, when you are not incarnated on the Planet Earth. I`m sure, you`ll remember how to be outside of the life.

I, in the other hand, feel everything as if it is a beautiful dream, and I know that this is a dream and that I am awake. Universe`s humor lies in the fact that the earthly incarnation is even more like a "dream" then the beyond, as people call the dreaming or the death, because only in life one can truly be awaken. To be awaken and see around you EVERYTHING! And when your life is a dream, then all the people`s dreams are The Co-creation—*the will*! But I'm outside of that Co-creation."

"Are there any better?"

"Depends on You," she replied. "The bliss can be felt equally in both cases. But on the Earth, one`s *will* is very fond of The Co-creation. One can feel and change anything on Earth, regardless of who you are."

"All are equal, right?" I had heard somewhere that wisdom.

"Yes," she spinned herself a few times. "Everybody can do what you do."

"Can everybody communicate with one`s guardian angel and visit other worlds?"

"Of course. And this is only the beginning."

Kathy picked up some snow and tried to throw it towards me. She failed to lift it.

"But why doesn`t anybody else do it?" I asked, noting that I`ve never heard my acquaintances do that.

Kathy reiterated her movements, and then looked at me and asked:

"Understand?"

Somewhy I started to laugh.

I often experienced it around Kathy, as if something had tickled my surroundings.

"It`s like I understand you, but with my perceptions," I said, still having the tickle-kind emotional feeling.

"You're more than your body. This is your energy, that tickles. This energy knows everything. I told you that I use your words, but I am merely reminding you, my dear, what you already know.

The fact that you are now talking to me, is that you *remember* how to do it. You chose it to your life, before taking this mission on Earth.

And I have chosen my own level in terms of what I can *remember*.

Well, every person have chosen its level according to where one wants to be. Just as he *remembers* himself, it *will* be the incarnation of his *intent*. And where is one's power of the *will* and effort, on that level one can be."

I took a handful of snow and threw it towards Kathy. We laughed, and looked straight up into the sky some time in silence.

"But how do you *remember* how to throw the snow?" I broke the silence of thoughts.

"I was a person once. A woman. So I stayed very close to that level, which was the point of my fondness of my soul," Kathy said very happily looking back into the past, and continued:

"We knew each other, Meckron. I was your soulmate's younger sister. You gave your life that day, to rescue mine, and I was touched and inspired by that so much, that I *willed* to be your guardian angel after that incarnation. And I have been one so far."

"What? When was this?"

The pictures from the past came to me, filling my vision.

"Ages ago," Kathy said and she was as cheerful as ever and she seemed to shine bluish light around her.

"But who was I in my previous life?"

"This knowledge would only bother you at this point. It comes to you later. For now—fix this life of yours at hand."

I was always stunned when communicating with Kathy. On the one hand, I was feeling an infinite peace and stability, and on the other, the realizations and the perceptions were storming inside me the way that I had to grab my hat with both hands or lose it like the bottle of champagne.

THE PRESENCE OF THE SHEPHERD

The spring had come.

I loved the smell of the first spring, the Sun heated those wonderful home-trees, which began, with a sigh of happiness, to collect greenery.

We were becoming close with Kathy. It has been several months, when I first heard her voice. One would have to believe that I will feel better in a daily basis, after the relationship with my guardian angel, but it was not so. Although the new and large-scale sensations were added to my perception, it made my 'everyday life' so much more depressing.

In the past, all my life seemed to be clear to me, as a Bible for Pope, but now I could not find an explanation even for the simple situations in my life. It seemed to me, as if I didn't control myself, watching myself as a spectator, as I did inappropriate things. It was like looking on "someone", who I earlier claimed as "myself", as it did stupid things.

Like that "someone" did not hear Kathy or didn't listen to me.

I consulted with my guardian angel:

"What the heck?! I cannot believe how stupid I can be sometimes!"

In response, I always heard a loving words:

"Dear Meckron, don`t blame yourself. This is what the Dark Forces are trying to make you. They work through the society's dark feelings. Some people call these dark feeling with the word—Ego. When we, Angels, are talking through your "Higher Self", then the Dark Forces are talking with your "Lower Self". And so it is for everyone."

"Can they make me do bad things?" I was worried.

"No. Just as I can not get you to do good things. And stop being so serious. Such seriousness is the field of an ego. A warrior-angel is gliding through the battles of his life, on his wings of the truth and humour," Kathy smiled.

I snort a laughter, but it did not change my concern over the situation.

"It's always only your choice, Meckron. It is always up to you!" Kathy continued. "You just have to learn to assemble yourself from the extent, from the spacefulness. Otherwise, all your lambs will run in a different directions, to look for better grass."

Kathy laughed and I realized that she is trying to make me not to fall into the deep hollows of concern.

"Did you just call me a sheep?" I also started to lighten up.

"Only if you can run this fast for the grass," my guardian angel was overwhelmed with laughter.

"Are the Dark Forces speaking with my lambs?"

"With some of them. Not all of them."

"What those Forces are telling to my lambs?"

"That your lambs would be better without you," Kathy said, as if she would try to tell the funniest story in the world with a straight face.

"But who am I then?"

"You are a Shepherd!" Kathy made a bow in front of the Shepherd as in the front of the king.

"What do these Dark Forces want from my sheep?"

"To trim them out of their coates!" Kathy said, and neither of us could no longer hold the laughter. I laughed out loud and the trees on my way home echoed back with joy.

"Do not let your lambs around the dark forest, there are wolves."

"Do I play my whistle, that they would not go?"

"Yes!" Kathy imitated the great whistle blower. "Play the echo out of the Universe!"

"What is my whistle?"

"The warrior-angel`s whistle is his humour and the choices of his soul—his *will*," was a definite answer.

I walked for a while thinking, forgetting my surroundings and my guardian angel.

One week went by.

There was a party in the school I went to. I used to go there to spend time with my friends.

Every conversation with Kathy seemed to alienate me from my previous "self". From that "self", which I was with my friends and with other people. For a long time I was feeling that I am pretending who I am with other people. Kathy`s appearence always made me a very alarmed about the surroundings. She made me very analyzing, in-controlling with the note of a humour and creativeness:

"How are your lambs?" I heard the voice by my side.

I leaned against the corridor wall, listening to the loud music upstairs. My friends were having a conversation about the life that started to become distant for me.

"I have a question," I replied. "Are those people, who I call friends, are my friends or the friends of the lambs?"

"Both," Kathy watched those around us. "Your lambs are the interpreters between your Higher Self and theirs."

"How do I . . . Kathy, I do not know how to communicate with them anymore."

"Use the language of a sheep", she laughed angelically and then imitating a sheep: "Baa-aa-a!"

I laughed and one of my friends asked me where the whole joke is at, but I didn`t reply.

Kathy looked at my friend with a warm compassion for a moment and continued:

"You could always talk with their Higher Self, as you talk with mine, but you can also use a language of a sheep. Just find a language they understand, but remember your efforts to help them."

At the same time, one of the friends invited me out to the school`s greenhouse to drink beer. My lamb knew its taste from before.

I went.

Kathy was talking to me on the way, and I noticed, that she was influencing the nightly fog around us with her motion:

"The alcohol is a drug. If you exaggerate, then you will have trouble hearing me."

"Ok. Thank you."

The desire to get rid of my lambs was increasing in me, as I saw my friends talk and act. I was fed up of faking an impressions, to make fool of myself doing stupid things with my friends, and the boundless snacking of the grass of the society.

Fortunately, the warm night of the spring was dark, as the bottle circled in the pack of my friends and when it was my turn, I just tipped the bottle on my lips, but didn`t swallow it. All had the impression that I drank with them along.

I felt very silly. Another stupid faked impression.

Kathy appeared next to me and nodded approvingly.

I turned to her in my mind:

"They do not want to know me as the Shepherd, they just want me to be a lamb and grow some wool."

"You can always talk to them as the Shepherd. When you're ready. Your mission on Earth is to awaken the other warrior-angels, it can only be done, through talking with their Higher Selves. Have some hope in them. One day you will speak freely and everyone's Shepherd will be awaken through your words."

I didn`t think it would ever happen. However, after that night I did not recognize myself anymore as a lamb, not at parties or anywhere else.

The center of my being was concentrated on something else, on something immeasurable and indescribable.

I did not understand anymore the pleasure of exaggeration and wasting the life, the recklessness and the un-purposeness.

I wanted to live my life as myself. As a warrior-angel.

Awakened. Right here, right now. I wanted to be a Shepherd, who will choose the grass for it`s lambs himself.

MANIFESTING THE WORLD

I spent a week, practicing the presence of the Shepherd.

Every day, my movements became more economical, more controlled, and it also happened with my speech.

It felt like my energy was directed to somewhere invisible, into non-daily life.

I felt how my energy level is rising, and not only in the body. My attention was constantly directed into thoughts, dreams and sensations, but not on the emotion-noise or everyday-rushing. I did my daily things, in a way of just like passing through—as in dreams.

"Is the Shepherd the one who rules over the *will of intent?*" I asked from my new friend on a warm sunny day, near the gravel road, throwing stones.

"Yes," said Kathy, my guardian angel, who was sitting on my right. "It is his field of action."

"And what is exactly the Shepherd?"

"The Shepherd is a point in the Universe, where the majority of your energy is concentrated. The Shepherd is an expression of the Soul."

"What is my energy?"

"In the "Simple Joe`s language", they are the qualities, which you master with your *will.*"

The newborn grass was swinging in the warm summer breeze. I felt the velvety freshness of the clouds in the petting winds.

"Meaning, I can manage my energies?"

"*Meaning*, for once you understood me?" Kathy laughed.

"*Meaning*, I can add the qualities and abilities to myself with my *intent*?"

"Yes, by all *means*. But that does not *mean* that you can get self-important by doing that."

"What's that supposed to *mean*?"

"It *means*, you thought, whether you could add yourself enough qualities to hit that telephone post over there? That was what you *meant*, right?"

Kathy pointed her finger at a tar black telephone post on the other side of a 80-yard greenful grass field.

"Enough with the *mean-game*. I already forgot, that you can read my mind," I said, thinking that she will let it go now.

Did she ever!

"Well, try it, oh grand warrior-angel!" she made a bow, as her hand was raised towards me, like they did in the times of fairytales.

I had thrown thousands of stones, but my accuracy was no better seen than that telephone post for me.

"Are you kidding me? No-one can hit that thing from here. It`s even more far away than my graduation," I laughed raising my brows.

But Kathy went on:

"You wanted to say, that no-one *wills* to hit that one?"

"Oh, come on . . ."

"I`m waiting," she was into her acts again, holding her hands crossed on her chest like a little spoiled kid, tapping her finger on the elbow.

I laughed. Then I slowly got up from the warm grass and chose a fit stone.

"Just *will* the stone to hit that post, instead of trying to do so. It`s important to hold your *will* on that intent, which focuses *the ray of soul*," Kathy explained.

"So I just need to *intend* it?"

"To *will* it and take the first step."

I shook my head. This will never work.

I intended wide and clearly that the stone would hit that old dark telephone pole and I saw it in my vision, where the stone will hit on that wooden post. I held the *will* on that image and threw the chilly bluish stone.

I saw how the stone flew in the sky, becoming smaller, and as it started to fell off it`s course towards the right target, it suddenly bended the trajectore!

It was bending towards the telephone post. I steared my mouth open like a tunnel, how the stone hit exactly that spot, which it had seen in the image of my vision. Then the sound of a contact of the stone and wood reached me.

"What in the name of a sweet sunshine . . ." I said these words in slow motion.

As I still drilled that high wooden pole with my eyes, the way that someone could make a sculpture of me, Kathy said:

"Everything in your life works this way," she explained and continued, "don`t forget it."

"Was that the work of the *will*?" I was still dazzeled.

"The *will*, concentration and an action," Kathy replied and smiled. "That is how you visit the other worlds too."

I had a lot of missions on my wall already, visiting *the other worlds* in out-of-body experiences.

"But I didn`t really believe, that I was the one who can hit the pole."

"Oh really?" Kathy asked and I knew this claim sounded like a baa-a of a lamb.

During the next few months I practiced the *will* on every occasion, hitting things with stones and *willing* and visualizing the qualities for myself like sense of humor or luck or great math skills. It really worked!

At night I practiced the *will* in my out-of-body experiences, on an "important missions" in the other realms, where I visualized the powers to myself and virtues to strenghten my *will*.

One night, I woke up in a ladies bath-room with my dreaming energy body or *the ray of soul* as Kathy calls it.

I saw how a blond young woman cried on the floor in anguish. I heared her thoughts like they were words as black birds filling my surroundings. They were desperate and suicidal thoughts.

I reached my hand and startled her, as I said:

"Come on. It`s for nothing . . . come on . . ."

I said it in some foreign language, maybe in french.

Slowly she took my hand and when I pulled her up, I felt a vortex and it woke me into the bed.

Kathy appeared beside me.

"Was that this realm?" I asked elated.

"Yes," she said. "Now she thinks she saw an angel, because you disappeared in front of her eyes. And by the sweet heavens! She`s right!"

Her jokes were always kind and warm.

"I hope she`s ok . . ." I said into my pillow and fell asleep. Something was added again in my being. People started to feel good around me. They actually started to like being with me.

Was I really starting to help people? Had I really started to *intend* it?

Was I really starting to manifest the world around me with the Light?

THE COMPETITION

I was in a classroom, sitting behind my old trusted visible desk with my new trusted invisible friend. The skinny teachess was talking about how important it is to be a more-achiever and to have better grades than others.

Or else we where aught to find ourselves in a stinking busstop, talking our stories to emptied liquer bottles. The only possible way to ever save ourselves and have a redemption, according to her, was to get better results than others, in school.

"You`ll never beat me," one of my classmates told me with his bored no-impressional face as a joke, just as I wanted to ask about it from my guardian angel.

"Actually I was having an epiphany. Do you mind?" I answered, joking too.

"By holy means, don`t let me stop you," my friend whispered kiddingly.

I turned to my cheerful angel, who was sitting on my desk:

"How do you call that stuff? Should I pay any attention at all?"

"I think you call it the competition," she smiled kindly and continued:

"There is a lesson to learn here."

"So should I be competing then?"

"The warrior-angel has a different point of view on that subject. Let me tell you a true story and then you can find the answeres for yourself.

In the middle of a pensive morning, the Sun sees how two children are walking on the road. Actually, only the girl with a bluish white linen dress is walking on the road, her agilitile little brother spends more time in a ditch, behind the trees, caressing them and running round and round around his beautiful sister.

The young brother says amain, clapping his hands:

"Let`s compete! I`ll race you to the grandmother`s house!"

"Oh, dear," she says. "Always competing and competing. Well alright. Let`s do it your way this time."

The little delectable brother stays still for a while, giving his sister kindly the head start, and then starts to run. In a while he passes by his walking sister and disappeares behind the curve, where the road was turning behind the forest.

The little brother runs a bit further before stopping, then looking back, whether his sister is cathing up with him or not.

But the girl with a bright dress is nowhere to be seen.

He runs further, to the next curve, resting there a bit on a big rock, waiting for his sister and wondering how much of the head start he has now.

So he is sitting and sitting there for catching a breath, and the Sun is fulfilling the champion with it`s rays and the master Wind is cooling him royally.

But the girl is seen on the no horizon.

The little boy is wondering:

"Oh, how can my sister be so slow. She won`t even beat the Sun riding on the sky, like this."

He decided to run back one curve, so her sister wouldn`t lose too immensely, but the girl is not there eighter.

Just standing there and scratching his head three times, he starts to run back to the first curve, thinking:

"I can bet my mood, that she should be definitely there already. After all, she isn`t a snail, who races the Day."

But when he got to the first curve—what a surprise—there was not even a warmness of the sister.

He shook his shoulders and ran to the grandma`s house, where they would get their first bear to help them in the household. He thought that he probably will see her there, when she finally gets there.

But as he arrived, he saw his sister, in her one hand—the red and black berries and the other hand—grandma.

"Where did you linger so long, my dear champion," the sister said. "Almost missed you enough to go seeking," she laughed.

"I was seeking for you! Two times I ran the path through, but you were on your own path, instead? Is that because you can`t beat me on mine?" the little out-of-breath boy smiled.

"It`s exactly how it is. But I, you see, knew that aint the competing an arduous job for even you, and I wanted your strenght to play with you until the evening, so here, I went to the forest and picked some berries for you," she said and continued:

"But you, dear Adin, are the two-time-champion on your divine path!"

The boy took the berries and said:

"And you on your path, Shenna."

THE HEALING HANDS

It was a very gorgeus summer, filled with creative aromas. Dry and warm july was a wonderful and talkative company on my spiritual walks.

Since I started to delve in myself as a Warrior-angel, these walks became crucial in my life. These walks gave me a chance to think—to feel that I walk my path, being the moment, being a Shepherd.

With wonderful soft clouds in the high blue sky and gratifying sun caressing everything, as I was walking.

I saw two kids riding on a bycicles on a blooming meadow path.

I was journeing on that path and suddenly I noticed a black beetle with beautifyl mild rainbow shine. The bisycle had run over it. I couldn`t tell if it was dead.

I decided to try.

Peacefully I looked the meadow waving around me in a warm kind wind, took the beetle gently to my left palm and held the other hand above it, where the broken beetle was lying.

I tried to heal it with the energies I had learned to control. I wanted so passionately, that she would live! I *willed* it from the bottom of my heart! The more I tried to help her, the more I started to love her. The first five minutes passed by, as I was trying to warm her with the light of my hands, and keep the vision of her healed and how she scud from my hands into the grass.

But still nothing.

I sat down, still concentrating, *willing*, intending, visualizing, healing. My affection against that beetle was already so deep, that through my tears I said:

"I am a child of the God. I *will* that this beetle would live. I`m not moving, before she is healed, or I am dead."

And I held the image of her healing in my mind, all the way, as Kathy had taught me.

Suddenly!

I felt the first movement on the palm of my hand. I continued doing whatever I was doing. I continued, until that beetle was scudding from the palm of my hand, into the green warm grass. This image was exactly like I saw it in my visualization. It was like a *deja vu*.

Through the tears of joy, I circled slowly, admirering my surroundings, saying:

"Thank you!"

As I returned from that journey, I suddenly felt not joy, but the unending sorrow, melancholy, resembling to a pain of a self-pity. I didn`t know where it came from, nor could I explain it.

Thinking that it was my weakness, I didn`t ask about it from my guardian angel, and she can`t answer if the question isn`t born.

This feeling haunted me for months, years, reappearing like a dark shadow. I used to cry because of the heavyness of that feeling.

Kathy didn`t interfere—it was my battle.

A few months later, I came across the first spiritual book, that I read with passion. This book not only explained the secrets of Allness to me, but confirmed every word that Kathy had told me. I felt it was the first book, where something important was said.

For my fortune, all my family was very spiritual, and this book was given to me by my dear mom. This wonderful book was called "Anastasia" by Vladimir Megre. I loved that book and admired what was said, because the words of that book filled me with energetic images, that was missing in me, for my guardian angel to explain the angles of the Allness to me.

As I acquired the Images of the Creation, I could speak with Kathy more precisely.

"Are these the Dark Forces, that give me these painful feelings?" I asked Kathy, when I was under this energetic attack once again.

"Yes," she said and continued, "their Dark Rays desire to stop the good, that you seek to achieve. But such a failure is not for a warrior-angel."

"What can I do to fight them?"

"Fill yourself with Virtues. The Dark feelings and the Virtues are all Energies. They have been there from the Beginning. They are intelligent and determined Beings. Your weak spots will always be the negative emotions, that you choose to let inside you, which opens the door to any of those Energies, those Dark Beings. Through those doorway particles, the Dark Forces can aim their destructing energy to you, if they want.

So if you feel anything but the state of love, the happiness, you should look into it and try to give rise to the loveful feelings. If that doesn`t work—try harder, until you master the state of love in every situation in life. The state of love is a normal state of a warrior-angel. In this case, the warrior-angel is empowered by the Forces of Light—the Virtues. To dwell intentionally in the heavy, dark feelings, in the self-pity or weakness or illusions of the egoistic needs, just won`t do. Giving up the concentration to feel the bright feelings, is not an option for a warrior-angel. So choose the Virtues. Always. In every second of your incarnation. No-one can choose it for you."

"Are you saying that I want to feel this way?"

Kathy made a surprised face, as if I had not heared anything she had told me. But she knew better.

"All that you see or hear or percieve in the world is what you choose to let inside you. If you choose to live in the atmosphere of the Energy of Love, it shall be so. It will manifest around you through the symbols of Love.

The Human Being is the only capable being in the Universe, who can choose between the Energies, who can balance them and control them. This is your mission for now on. So get your feathers together and show them what a warrior-angel can do!"

"The Energy of Love . . . My soulmate!" I whispered.

The image of my beloved person, my dear soulmate, was always the source of the light for me. My hope and my prize. The dream of meeting her, was the way my life was supposed to be and she was my strenght and inspiration for whatever I came to do in this incarnation.

I always dreamed about her—my other half—I wanted to do what`s right because she would love me this way. I wanted to be a good person, because she would love me as a good person.

"I will give my best to help people, even if my soulmate is far away and doesn`t see what I do."

"That`s better, but is that your best?" Kathy asked.

I felt a bit better and I could fall asleep.

I woke up, being out of my body.

There was a dark room and we were standing on the cold pavement of the last stairs to that room with the dark-skinned female warrior shaman.

I knew that woman, but I couldn`t remember her. We was going to another spiritual mission, but we fell off course. Ahead of us, there was a throne room with smaller and bigger candles. As a warrior-angel, I "knew" this place.

"Quick! Get out!" I turned motionlessly to my friend, slowly raising my hand to cover her retreat, as she backed off the same way we came in.

In that room, I saw a weird shape appeared, like a shape of a man, but it didn`t resemble to a human being with anything else.

"Come on over to our side," his words sounded from the different angles of that room.

As an Angel, I knew that it was the Leader of the Dark Forces and that he can`t fight me or damage me, because of who I am. Because of I am "me". A warrior-angel. A Human Being.

"No," I said. "I have decided."

He started to propose some riches and powers for me, but I just left, returning into my body.

I called my guardian angel, when I saw my peaceful room.

"Kathy!"

With an instant, she was at my side. It seemed a few hours had passed.

"I think I made someone angry just now," I laughed.

My guardian angel laughed with me:

"Don`t worry. He`s always angry," and continued with a note of seriousness:

"You have the Healing Hands. Your Light is a Blessing Light. Anyone who will open their way of life the way that you have done, will activate one`s *ray of soul.* You use it to travel in the other worlds and this one and to help others. Learn to *aim* your *ray of soul.*"

"When will I learn it and where and how?"

"Just use it. Here and always."

I started to use *the ray of soul* on other people, to discover it further. I chose one of the most depressed and confused and broken person I could find, who had a blood cancer, broken heart and the worst of all—a teenage youth, like I had.

We were talking through the internet and I tried to aim *the ray of soul* on her and explained a few of the life secrets that Kathy had taught me.

She had taken the pills for years, but now, as she went to the doctor after two weeks, the sickness was disappeared without a trace, as it had been a wrong test. A mistake.

"You did something, didn`t you? What? How?" she asked me.

"I just sent the Divine Blessing Light to you, by aiming *the ray of soul.* Everyone can do it, you just need a *will* to do it."

I don`t know if she believed me or understood, but I believed in my *ray of soul.*

A few years ago, before I met my guardian angel, I was myself in a peril because of my so-called "weak heart", but now the symptoms had disappeared like the raisins in a white bread. One of my big helpers at that age, was a spiritual healer, near my birth place. She was trying to tell me the same thing that Kathy did and I took it as my moto through the childhood: "You need to respect and love everything around you. Everything around you is good for you for something. Defend it."

As it turned out, the so-called "weak heart" was the blocked energy in my heart chakra.

My body was strong and agilitile again, as I noticed after acquireing the *art of the will* and practicing *the ray of soul*. I could even project an unnatural speed and strenght and accuracy at some times.

Kathy told me that the only unnatural thing about it was my nack not to know anything about myself.

"To heal others, you must be healthy yourself," Kathy said and continued, "because to heal someone you should teach health."

I had no desire to be a healer. I still struggeld in sweat end tears and pens to graduate and get into a high-school. A part of me still wanted to be like everybody else.

"Not only the body shows the health of the person," my guardian angel said. "To be a healthy person, your body, thoughts, dreams and life has to be healthy. You know that the Human Being lives mostly on a three Realms of Being—the physical realm, the spiritual realm and the realm of the soul. Plus the sub-realms of an individual choosing.

All these realms must be Enlightened by your Light. The healthy person can not allow the dark places in his space, especially a warrior-angel."

"I know—I have to give my best, right?"

"Exactly," she said. "Give and take the best of you."

THE SHIELD OF LIGHT

I felt strange on that day. It was like something was colliding around me, then building up. I felt the scent of the magnets as I was walking in the sun of a young summer.

I had met a girl, who had an unusual dream, that caught my attention. She was 16-year old friend of mine, with dark brown hair and eyes. Her mom was russian, so her name was Marina.

In the dream of hers, she saw that she was an oracle in the past, and that she died over and over again because of it. She didn`t know what to think of this dream.

"Her grandmother was a witch, a healer," Kathy said and continued, "that is why she has enough energy to remember her past lives. Ask her about her grandmother."

I did as my guardian angel suggested.

"Marina, was your grandmother a witch?"

"Nice," Kathy laughed. "Very subtle."

It was a sore subject to that girl. Her family was embarrassed because of their ancestor and they never spoke about it. It was like a family secret, that you don`t tell to anyone. Like a skeleton-in-a-closet kind of matter.

"What!?" Marina asked. "How can you know that?"

She didn`t like my question, because she was raised in a "civil way", not to believe anything as such. Her parents even forbitted her talking with her grandmother as she got older.

"I have my ways to know," I said, having no intention to tell her about my world and who told me this.

"Are you one of them? Did they sent you?" she was angry at me.

"One of who?"

"One of his guys. Did he put you up to this? What do you want?"

"It`s just a question. Your grandmother taught you spells and wards when you were a child, didn`t she?"

I asked it on a behalf of my guardian angel`s advise.

"He can`t know that, how can you?!"

She was very upset.

"Because I`m here to help. Who is he?" I referred to that mystery someone, starting to have an idea why I met this girl.

"So you`re not one of them? Then . . ."

"So tell me about them?" I asked.

"I don`t know. I haven`t told about it to anyone. I`m scared," she held back and suddenly spilled it out like by an accident:

"I threw a mob money into the river!"

She raised her hand to her lips. I was silent for a moment.

"Now how does anyone manage to do that?" I laughed.

"I know, it`s crazy. Just like in the movies, right? I`m so stupid. I just didn`t want him to be involved with such things."

"Who?" I scratched my neck.

"My boy-friend. I met him a month ago. I think he is going to kill me, as soon as he finds out. I really think he will. I wish I had never met him. I was thinking of killing myself, cuz I can`t take this anymore . . ."

I looked at Kathy. She looked back at me as it was my decision.

"I can help you," I said. "It will be ok."

"How?" she asked. "You don`t even live around here. He can come anytime."

"The same way I knew about your grandmother. I can protect you. Just stay home and don`t worry."

The next day I was walking on the flowery road of my home meadows, 300 miles away from Marina.

Suddenly I started to lose my sight and all went black and I sat down.

I woke up a few minutes later, thinking it was the blood pressure.

On that evening I spoke with Marina through the live messenger in the internet.

"What did you do?" she asked me.

"What happened?" Kathy showed up on my right, when I typed this question.

"I`m not sure. I went to a store and they waited for me behind my house. My boy-friend was one of them. They asked me where the money was. I said I threw it away. They didn`t believe me and tried to grab me to take me with them. As my boy-friend stepped a few steps towards me, it seemed something pushed him back. The other two made their move too, but it was just like stepping against the imaginable wall. They just walked away like under some kind of a spell or confusion. I haven`t seen them since."

And she never did again.

"Was that you?" she asked with a note of gratitude.

"What time did it happened? Around six?"

She said yes.

I turned to my guardian angel. Kathy explained, that it was The Shield of Light, created by Marina's present guardian angels and me. She also said that every Human Being is able to create something similar, with *the ray of soul.* Every human on the planet is a magical being, with the special powers. One just needs to discover them as one of the talents one has. Just to be concentrated in a moment with a pure form of one's state of being, and then one would be amazed what a Human Being can do and how good one can do it.

She explained further, that I didn't remember what I did, because I still don't have enough energy to recollect everything that I see with my *angelic form,* which I have between the incarnations and outside of a daily world. And that is why I don't remember every dream at night. Such abilities can be upgraded and practiced at night when our energies are in the form of *the ray of soul.*

"So was that you?!" Marina repeated her question.

"I helped," I said and told her what happened to me around six and what my guardian angel told me about it.

"Your guardian angel?" she was overwhelmed. "The Shield of Light? *The ray of soul?* Is that all real?!"

She seemed to be joyful, hearing about this kind of things from someone else. She had pushed her own supernatural experiences aside, locked them deep inside, where she had put her grandmather too.

"Go to her," I said. "Go to her and tell your grandmother about it. You will know where to go from there."

"Thank you! I don't know who you are or where you came from . . . but thank you so much!"

She was very happy.

"I am a warrior-angel," I said to her. "This is what I do."

THE TWO WORLDS

The high-school.

Everyone who`s been there, hears these words differently, than the mere mortals, who untouchably of that battle, have only heard a lifechanging legends about it.

"It`s good for you, Meckron," said Kathy.

"I don`t know why I`m here. To whom I want to prove what?"

"It`s fine, it`s fine . . ." said my guardian angel melodically. "Maybe you can help someone here. It can`t be worse than a realm of Hell, where you fought a curse-dragon."

"Yeah, but I had a sword back there . . ." I answered and a passing student nudged me out of the way.

"At least they are not gonna let you get full of air," Kathy added. "There is a lesson here."

"You always say that," I noted.

"And we`re always right. We are the Messengers. Google us," she joked about her kind.

"A good one. So what`s the lesson then?" I asked.

"I suggest you to stay in high-school, until you have developed a sense of humor about yourself and your life. You are takeing yourself too seriously. If one takes oneself`s Ego too seriously, they end up living in a Hell. Yes. The

Hell can be present on the Earth. With the iron grip of the Ego, all you feel is pain and fear. Everything in your life will bring you sorrow or disappointment, anguish of feeling that nothing is good enough and the self-importance will control your choices through fear. Everything you get, achieve or lose will bring forth the worst emotions possible, because all in your life is based on a fear because of the need of control that comes from taking yourself too seriously. Most of the people are in the trap of these creatures who made that prison, and those beings do not like it, when someone tries a "prison-break"."

"Jesus, Kathy. It`s just a high-school."

She laughed over the shiver that ran down my spine, that was made by the unknown forces that didn`t want me to start to be free.

"Good. I think I hit the spot," she said and happily continued, "the warrior-angel is in control of his own feelings and choices and nothing can control them for him—not the situations, achievements, other beings or a rainy day on a picnic. He achieves this freedom through the Faith. The Faith into the Light—into The Way of the Allness. That means, that a warrior-angel trusts every second of his incarnation and never takes it too seriously, because it changes with every second. He knows that everything he does, is seen in the Universe by billions of spectators, but he also leaves himself a lightfulness, because he *feels* the Way of the Allness, which manifests through ease. A warrior-angel glides through the battle-field on the soft Lightful Wings of the Humor."

We entered into a classroom with my guardian angel and saw a bunch of people I didn`t know.

"The self-importance is the least of my problems here."

I had read about the ancient priests, who co-operated with these creatures, used the Energy of the Image to model the societys way of life and how they ruled the Earth, diminishing the freedom and lowering the natural abilities of people. With it, reducing Man`s divine qualities like the Speed of Thought, Spirituality and the Substance of a Live Images under the use of *the divine will.*

If there is something describing fully how to extract a Man from the Knowledge of the Source, splitting all the Truth into a little school subjects, abducting a Mankind from what is truly important, by directing people to seek the knowledge outside, rather than inside and to beg everything from outside, not to be a Creator by oneself, who is willing to Give, and with it making a prison of fear and taking that fear too seriously, then it`s a highschool.

Luckily, I had my guardian angel at my side, who speared me from the brainwash, because she was the silent voice for me, who spoke about what`s truly important and that the warrior-angel must stay true to his path, or else his incarnation will mean nothing.

"Don`t forget, that although a warrior-angel can not always choose the situation, because he will be there where they need him the most, but he can always choose *how* he is in that situation. You are here to understand the situation what the Mankind is up against, so you could help them later on," Kathy said.

"Ok, I`ll be here, trying to understand and do good. The part of me, which wanted to be like everybody else is starting to dissolve anyway. I would really want that the Mankind would be on a path of a Free Will, not on a path of fear that is represented here."

"On that case, dear Meckron, you have to become free yourself."

Now I knew what Kathy meant by that. On one hand, I was aware of society`s downfall, and the other, I didn`t understand in full the invisible mechanisms of my life, thanks to what my "social me" syndicated with the wants of the ego traps, that was encrafted into me by a negative worldviews and Images.

"You have been building your life for 17 years, according to this Era. To change extremly fast at once, would bring a disharmony," Kathy explained. "Step by step, dear Meckron, I will help you. We`ll laugh one day, looking back on that lesson, I assure you."

And then there was the schoolwork.

Luckily I didn`t have a hard time in my schoolwork, because I started to speak at the age of 1, learned how to read at the age of 4 and had a piano lessons at the age of 6. In addition, Kathy had taught me to become invisible when they ask students in class.

"Turn your light off and don`t make an eye contact—it aims *the ray of soul*," she said.

Plus I had a kind of a photographic memory, that gave me a possibility to close my eyes and re-read the page I memorized, when the schooltest was encountered.

Even so, I rather engaged into an analysis of the situation, then in the school material—I didn`t think those letters they called "grades", were more important than the buns in the school cafeteria.

But my "social me" was still intact, which made me feel incredibly lonely, depressed, limited and worthless because that is what that place was trying so hard to do through the "social me"—make that part a socially controlled one. I understood that this was the battle ahead, that Kathy told me about.

I realized—all the students there felt that way underneath, knowingly or not. But everyone didn`t hear his guardian angel, to have an explanation over this. And so they have a wonderful endeavor to the better future, unknowing where their sadness and secret anxiety of imprisonment lies.

One day I made a descision:

"Kathy!"

She suddenly was sitting next to me in the school cafeteria, on the red soft chair at my right.

"That`s enough, Kathy. I understood. The system is trying to control you, when you don`t control your own life. If you don`t have a Blissful Image of the Way of Life, walking on the right path of your soul. This is what the Dark Forces are trying to do, to block that image into the Human Being through this system. If you don`t create that Image, it will be done for you."

Kathy nodded.

"What about the lesson? Any news from the other side of a barbed wire?"

A dressed black student wanted to sit on the chair where Kathy was sitting, but he somehow sensed her presence and chose another chair.

"I will leave this school now and make the Blissful Image of my Way of Life, starting to walk a path of a warrior-angel, helping others, teaching, supporting, loving them. And doing it on the soft Lightful Wings of the Humor."

My guardian angel seemed to be very satisfied, but said nothing.

"Want a bun?" I asked her.

"No, thank you," she said. "I`m on a special diet."

I stayed into that school a few weeks, enjoying the new-found freedom that I was blessed with. The models of the society didn`t weigh on me anymore, nor did they make me act as programmed. I realized I wasn`t in a prison anymore.

When others shaked in fear for oncoming tests, loosing sleep over a grade, and sit on their chairs like on a hot stove, I brought them snacks from the caffeteria with smiles.

When others turned into a stone in the reign of a terrory geography teacher, I was coloring a picture that one of the first-graders gave me, and when the interrigation catched me, I claimed that I wasn`t listening and went on with my intriguing endavour. It really is a wonderful piece of activity! I enjoyed it a lot.

The seemingly strict teacher was programmed by that same system that tried to slave everyone else too, so she didn`t have a reaction programmed to deal such creative action, so she ignored me as "the flaw of the system", and so did my classmates.

I had a wonderful and unforgettably fun time there, helping others, making them feel better and with every possible step, trying to awake them from this hibernation. To help them out of that prison of fear. But it has to be a free choice, to be free.

Finally!

I was free! I was alive! I was a warrior-angel and percieved every moment with joy.

When the system couldn`t control me anymore, the Dark Forces sent their agents to attack me directly and to test me. Probably that was exactly what my guardian angel was telling me about.

I was walking towards the bus station, after school. Someone with the God-given humorous logic had built the school next to the cemetary. Nice!

On the road, there was other students too, pounding the springful road to home after school, but my attention was attracted by a young girl.

She looked like a 7-year-old young girl with a dark hair and weird clothes. No-one else seemed to notice that girl, even if she was passing by them, and she steared at me all the way without blinking. I felt my bones freezing and a cold shiver run down my spine, when she was closing. Her head was bent on the side and her walk was cryptic. Her footsteps filled my ears as she got closer and closer with every step.

Her motionless bottomless glass doll-eyes were stearing right at me without a look inside them, just with a mocking grin on her face.

Other senior students seemed to move out of that little girls way, like being unable to "register" her in their attention. I had seen something like that on the missions in the other worlds, out of body, and thanks to those experiences, I felt like something powerful landed in me.

I felt myself as being out of my body, with the ray of soul, just like on those missions. I didn`t change my step, I walked right to her. I was ready to fight, but I wanted to see what she will do. When she was almost passing me by, she suddenly hit me right to the left ribs with her cold fist. The hit was so strong, that I couldn`t breath for a second and also the hit took my vision for 1-2 seconds. I turned around quickly, ready to use the Light Blast on her, but she was gone. The road was empty. Only some students walked towards me from the distance. That was the first time I encountered an agent of the Dark Forces. A flesh demon.

What was weird about it that time, was that I forgot the incident for years. I lived as a warrior-angel, improving myself humorously, trying to put the two worlds together and combining my experiences into my daily life.

Kathy gave me all sorts of practices, for instance—star-gazing. She said that it is the fastest way to purify my energies.

And she wanted me to put my palms behind the ears and to listen the surroundings. It was really fun, because it gave me a wonderful realization, how much I actually missed around me. At the beginning I started to sneeze during this training. Kathy said it was because of the balance of the senses—if one is enhanced, the others try to keep up, and that the smelling is one of the most energetic senses we have.

I even graduated high-school, later on, because I wanted to test myself on the levels of spirituality and the lightfulness and humor, as the warrior-angel greets all the challenges with honor and praise. Especially the hard challenges.

But the meeting with the demon on the daily realm I couldn`t combine with my life, until later on, when I was more evolved on the energetic level.

It came to me, when I was realizing more and more, that it`s all the same—my daily life and the missions in the other worlds and my guardian angel. It`s all here. Right now. It`s happening!

After I traveled with *the ray of soul* hundreds of times and met spiritual masters, dream-seers, angels, the past and future, the two worlds started to melt together slowly—the daily world and the world of a warrior-angel.

CHAPTER TWO:
"SPREADING THE WINGS"

BETWEEN THE MOON AND THE EARTH

I was always waiting for the night. I liked the night, first because of its marvelous mysteriousness, because the world is something else at night, and second, because I loved to travel with *the ray of soul.*

At one night, I woke up in a beautiful world. In another world. I looked into the sky and I saw stars and at the same time—the sun. The sky was different mostly because there was the Moon and the planet Earth at the same time.

Suddenly.

From the distance, I saw a boy in a taoistic clothes, whose bold head shined like a glittering sea. The whole world was a bit hazy, like the eyes were full of a soft light. I had a taste of the nectar in my mouth, because there was a lot of flowers in that world.

There he was scurrying, that little boy, into a little building that reminded me a shed, like he was trying to hide from someone. I thought he might be in trouble.

I ran into the same shed-like building and saw a boy. He looked at me with his warm eyes, with a relief. After me, a man entered, one of the three men with flabby clothes. I stood between him and the boy, protecting him. The man in a gray clothing used some martial arts against me, and I responded. When I punched him away with a wind-like energy, the all three retreated.

I was back in my bed.

"Kathy, these missions are making me hungry."

"Of course, you are using the energy. The life-force is the one that helps to overcome the barriers of the worlds."

She was sitting on the floor.

"I was . . . where?" I asked.

"Between the Moon and the Earth," she said and continued, "there is a world, a world resembling to this one, with the Spiritual Laws, but the energy isn`t so dense and the light also. That is why the people of this Era can`t see it with their eyes. Just like they can`t see the fairies and elementals anymore, though every day they are present around them."

"What`s going on there, into that world?"

"There the Living Images are formed and purified. The Living Images, that are born in the mind of a living Human Being."

"But, Kathy, are my Living Images seen there too, like I saw that taoist boy?"

"Everything is seen to everyone, Meckron. To those who has a specific pureness, to *see* understandably. It`s like a code that opens the Images for you. They will open according to the vibration of your thoughts and feelings. Your vibration is a password. If your vibration is equal to the vibration of the selected Living Image, then you can see it, understand it and even change it. The Great Warriors of Spirit are resting in the world between the Moon and the Earth. This realm will heal your soul, spirit and even your bodies, if you are worthy to the pureness of that realm."

"Bodies?" I asked half-dozy.

"A Human Being has a lot of bodies. Which one a Human Being uses, depends on where one`s attention is aimed."

"What kind of bodies?"

"Some of them are more dense than others," she said. "Between the Moon and the Earth, you can use the different types of bodies. The important thing is, that you would possess the bright feelings. The Virtues.

Then the Forces of Light are with you, and the Light will keep your bodies together, the beautiful Light that manifests through the warming energies of your Dream."

"I dream so warmly, that the world would be a place, where all the people could live for all eternity in the nature of Paradise, so they would possess the creation-abilities like our Dad does, and that they would have a forever-loved soulmate, with whom to share the Blessing Light of your wise and kind divine way of life."

I got up from the bed and scampered outside, into the warm bath of the blissful morning rays of sun. I listened to an astonishing song of the free birds, diving in the sky and the Light of the Energy of Love, mirrored from the Sun, fulfilled the space between my particles, in this wonderous materialized Dream of our Eternal Dad.

"Your dreams are creating the future with His Dream. The realm of the Living Images holds the light in itself, and doesn`t reflect it. It is given this way, so through the Free Will of a Human Being, the visible Living Image would manifest through one`s path."

I looked into the bottomlessly blue sky, how the sweet clouds were sailing, while standing on the cushy grass on my bare feet.

"I understand," I answered smiling. "This is why it is so blissful to be . . . just be . . . and feel that your dreams are stored safely somewhere. Somewhere over the rainbow. Somewhere between the Moon and the Earth."

THE GIFT OF THE SILENCE

Communicating with my supporting guardian angel, I started to speak less and less with those, who sat by my side at school, but lived in another world by another rules. Not by the Rules of a Warrior-angel.

In some point of that time I realized, that I have hard time to say anything to others, if they don`t know what I know.

I understood, how hard it must been for Kathy to talk to me, when the images behind the words I knew, were weak or not sufficient, with which I would understand the Entirety of Being, the Blessing and the endless incarnation of the Living Images through the Free Will.

"If you don`t have anything to say, that eighter heals, helps or empowers others, then it is better for you not to speak at all," said Kathy on a windless caressing day, when I was climbing to the top of a spruce tree.

"Jabbering isn`t my problem for a long time already. I think I have babbled enough for the thousand radios, in the past. What an amount of energy it might be . . . Fortunately, I am more economic now. At least because of the fact that I can`t tell anyone about a Real World that is around us. About what`s eternal and how the Energy of Love, who is a thinking, feeling, divine being, helps us to incarnate the Living Images through the Light of our Dreams."

"Yes, you can tell them about it," said the angel, sitting on the opposite branch of that tree. "You`re just not ready yet. One day you will tell them about the most wonderous world, the most real one, about the road to the Enlightenment. And about the world that will be for the joy of every living being. And you will awaken others like you, the other warrior-angels. But for now, it is very important for you to learn when and what to say."

"Another warrior-angel training, right?"

Kathy laughed glimmerly:

"It`s so sweet that you call it that way!"

We laughed together and then she continued:

"Start with the knowing when to be silent."

"Is now a good time?"

"Angels do speak silently . . ."

"But what is it good for, Kathy?"

"First," she raised her hand and started to count on her fingers the way, as if for sure no-one has enough fingers for that, "when you are silent, people will hear their own thoughts. It is most important, for them to designate the place of their Attention in the Allness."

"I understand. They have to feel them as a "*real self*", or their *will* is broken," I nodded.

"Yes. Secondly—never, ever, under no circumstances, disturb other people thinking."

"I understand. I shouldn`t break their Living Images or analysis."

"Good. And thirdly—speak only when you feel that someone is appointed to you with a lesson, asking you whether silently or out loud a question, and is ready to accept your Light and the Vibration."

"I understand. Everyone doesn`t want to be like me."

Kathy made her eyes big of the acted surprise:

"I think you have started to use your ability to evolve," and we both burst into laughter.

"But what if I will do otherwise?" I asked.

"Then, dear Meckron, you use violence and have to be responsible for the consequences of oncoming battle. Every word of a warrior-angel means a world. If you are incarnated as one, you represent our Universal Dad, the God. I know, dear Meckron, He has always been your role model and you love Him and miss him so much, this is seen for everyone."

"Yeah . . . and He doesn`t talk often . . ." I smiled, hasting silently. I missed Him so much.

"Why do you think He does that?" Kathy asked.

And the silent caressing wave of the warm wind touched the understanding tear on my cheak.

THE BLISSFUL IMAGE OF THE WAY OF LIFE

I had finally found myself.

I was living in a marvelous isolated forest house, that was located next to an ancient fir forest. On the back of the house, the merry little stream was musmuring and the light brown young deers with the white funny bottoms went eating apples under the old appletree at the east side window of that house at winters.

On this summer afternoon I was lying on my bed to go traveling with *the ray of soul*, to search The Blissful Images of the Way of Life.

I floated over the Siberian cedar-tree forests of a taiga. Into my view of counciousness, the small foresthouse was lighting up on the brightgreen glade of forest. The surroundings was remarcably clean and pure to the core, and the silent peace was floating in the atmosphere around that house, according to the purity of the thoughts that lived there.

I was closing up to that building, invisibly, floating through the window.

Inside the house, there were a lot of artful handmade equipment, placed with the thoroughly councious way and care. On the floor, there were the clean handmade colorful carpets and cozy milieu. Everything was hand-made and with incredible care and mastery.

In one part of the house, there was no household things, only a comfortable bed with an artistic sheets with linings.

On that bed, I saw an old man in a linen clothes, meditating in a white-golden bluish glow. On that instance, as I concentrated my ray of soul to him, he suddenly opened his eyes and looked right into me, reading me like a book. This energy-surge hit me back into my body, while it was resting in the warm rays of sun, in my bed.

I got up and went for a walk. It was a lovable summer day.

I thought to myself, how wonderful can be a Human Being`s life, looking back at what I saw. So harmonic, perfect and divine.

"Is that really the most important thing?" I turned to my guardian angel with a question. "That the Child of God would have the Living Engrained Home, through which he reigns the Universe?"

"Yes," Kathy said, floting left of me and trying to imitate the walking, "this is the plan of the Bright Forces, to bring the Humans back to the garden that He created."

"But a lot of people like the technocratic world," I was remembering the way of life of today`s society. "Will that end?"

"People will replace it with something even better. They will replace it with something, that is not based on the taking the Creation into pieces. Unfortunately, it is planned so, by the Dark Forces, that no human could stay on that level of the speed and purity of the thoughts, to overlook the situation and analyze it. Everyone are busy serving the system, that was made a long time ago, to get the society at the point that it is on your time.

To overcome the system, everyone should have a divine place, a temple of soul, a little place of the paradise that supports him or her—the Living Engrained Home for the parents and the children. For your lovely divine children!

A sacred place, where the superficial bustle and the illusions wouldn`t tear the Child of God from what matters the most. It is a good thing, if that place is in the pure environment. If it is not, then it has to be made pure.

It is important, that a Child of God would plant a tree there, that one likes. When the nature of that place cradles and recognizes the Child of God, then one can analyze and create without the influence of the Dark Forces, what his or her purpous enlights and how one could use everything that is, for the greater good, when one will combine it with the Blissful Image of the Way of Life."

"What is the foundation of that Blissful Image?"

"The Endeavor of the Soul. The knowing, to whom you sense to become and what is your outcome in the Light."

I had created the Blissful Image of the Way of Life, that has given me an amounts of joy, peace of mind and the richfulness of heart.

I had planted a cedar tree into the place I grew up, where I often sat on my own, thinking.

In that Image, I was living in the Living Engrained Home, with my soulmate, where the wonderful plants and trees were growing and our happy divine children lived.

"What should one concentrate the attention on, when creating the Blissful Image of the Way of Life?" I asked Kathy and visualizing the day when I will share my knowledge with other warrior-angels and with all the people.

"First," she sat on the big warm stone with a dry moss, "a person should concentrate one`s attention on the feelings, that one would like to feel in the life, as the life would only consist of a one moment. A person should induce the various feelings, find the likeable ones and determine them."

"Right."

"After that, a person should concentrate one`s attention to the other people, who is touched by that Image, and how they feel. Again, looking the eternity through a compressed scope of a moment."

"Yes."

"And finally, a person should concentrate one`s attention to that compressed moment of those feelings, how and if it lasts after 100 years, 1000 years, in eternity of the moments."

"Can you clarify?" I couldn`t understand her thoroughly.

"If a person thinks about a non-lasting pleasure, like a fame, riches, possessions—the things that will end in one`s lifetime or sooner, it will surely create a blast-like vibration, but it is followed by the vacuum-effect. All that seemed to shine, will consume it`s shine again, which it gave to the surroundings, by itself. Through that, the motion is still, like nothing happened. But when our Dad created the perfect tree, which`s outcome was a seed for another perfect tree, then His Creation incarnates the Light that was emanated, subscribing itself into the Eternity, giving infinity of that joy to everyone, which He felt on the moment of the creation of that perfect tree. Every one of you can stretch the moment of your own creation like that."

"And we can use the present Creation too?"

"Yes. And it is called the Co-creation. That is what our Dad awaits from His wise Children, the Co-creators. He kindly awaits, that His children would smile in the burst of inspiration, and through the Energy of Love, supported by

His Dream, creating their own Blissful Image of the Way of Life.

Then, every person—a Child of God—can be in contact with it`s parents—The God and the Energy of Love. These loveful parents happily lay the table of the eternity for their amazing Children, awaiting gently, silently hoping, that one day these Divine Children will be like them or more."

"Just like an old man in the cedar-forest?" I asked.

Kathy smiled and shined bright-bluish, as I felt the answer to that question with the silence flowing into me.

CONTROLLING THE THOUGHTS

"You will need the mastery in a one more subject in your amazing life," my guardian angel said, as we were standing on the bridge, under which a silent stream rippled.

I was leaning on the brown warm handrail of the handmade wooden bridge.

"Not that it`s the last one," I answered.

"It`s very important for the warrior-angel," Kathy smiled and continued, "that you know how to control your thoughts—eighter guide them or stop them."

I had concentrated a skyfull amount of energies into my thoughts for the last months, I thought that she said it, so I wouldn`t overdo it.

"I`m not controlling my thoughts?" I asked, knowing the importance of my thoughts.

"When you were at school, how frequently did you think about acting by the normal standards or by the expectations of someone or how to resolve dilemmas of emotions which were bound to your way of life?"

I took a deep breath of a warm sweet humid air, full of divine nectar of flowers.

"I think there's no need for answer, because you see everything that goes on in my life."

"I asked this, so the answer could bloom from inside of you. As you know, it's not really an example of controlling your thoughts—your school years."

"But, Kathy, who controlled my thoughts then, if it wasn't me?"

"The one who visualized such circumstances of the way of life and the emotions that came with it."

"It means, someone else controlled my thoughts. Ok. And with it, he could control what I was doing and what my life was like, right? But where did they came from, these alien-controlled thoughts?" I asked, seeing how a little blue bird winged itself to a branch, to take a peek.

"From the emotions, turning into them."

"What do you mean?"

"Your life is like this rippleing stream right here," Kathy pointed on a cooled waves of a glittering stream, that flowed under us abundantly and opulently.

"Your thoughts are that glitter, which you see, being in a moment, being a spectator with a point of view. Your thoughts reflect the Light. Emotions, on the other hand, are these stones in a stream or branches, that makes the water undulate. At the moment of those ripples, you see eighter Light on the peak of the waves or the bottom of the water—the axis of your worldview."

"Flowing statement. How can I control . . ." I started to ask that question, but the answer already was born inside of me. "The control over the emotions are the key to control my thoughts?"

"Yes," she said joyfully. "It's like these branches and stones on the bottom of that stream were yours to command. But there is no need to throw all of them out of the stream."

"I should displace them?"

"The bottom of that stream is yours to design, when you use the Thought, where and when and which emotions you want to feel."

"Kathy, you said before, that the Thought can be stopped. Why is that necessary?"

"Come with me," she made a gesture.

We walked away from the steady bridge, to the upstream, and then downstream. In some places there was seen the glitter of the light on the waves, in some places the trees consumed the light, laying a shadow on a stream.

"That bridge was the present moment—your present point of view about the stream, about the life. Stopping the thoughts will get you out of that perspective. Away from the bridge. That gave us a chance to step away from the flow, to take a glimpse to the upstream and the downstream—the past and the future. That different perspective gave you a chance to see what shadowed the light that touched the stream, to see the branches and the stones, that affect the flow. The Flow never stops, but stopping the Thought—it is a mastery of perspective, that governs you the Freedom of the Creation and Analysis."

"What is the result of stopping the Thought?"

Kathy asked me to close my eyes and take a stone from the stream and *relocate* it.

I closed my eyes, without choosing a stone. I stood there for a while. Then suddenly something wonderful happened!

I *heared* the ripples of the stream! Before I closed my eyes, I had only noticed a few stones in the stream, but now I heard hundreds of them, where they are located and I heared a kind of a symphony of that variation. I took a stone, using my hearing.

"Now throw it where the stream makes a curve."

I threw it and on the sound of the stone hitting the stream, I opened my eyes.

"Welcome to the Meditation!" Kathy laughed. "This is the result of stopping the thoughts."

I laughed with her, being overwhelmed with the simplicity and clarity of the Laws of the Universe.

"But how does it serve us in the bigger picture?" I asked.

"When you feel the Allness outside of the point of view—the perspective—you are able to *hear* everything that happens in the stream or out of it—on the meadows and forests and in the sky. But the main reward of the meditation is the purity and flowfulness of the stream—your life."

The muddy water reached us, from where I threw the stone.

Kathy asked me:

"What do you think, Meckron, where to this spring is heading?"

"To the sea?" I answered in an asking way.

"Back to the beginning—to the Source," she smiled.

THE ENERGETIC FIELD

I had learned to silence my noise of the thoughts, going into the meditation and regained some of the control over them.

When knowing how to silence the self-dialog of the ego, my energies started to balance, my chakras were starting to heal.

The senses about the situations, the people and all the other things, were magnifying. The feeling what`s good or bad was a lot more clearer and brighter.

In the old times, I hadn`t took advise from this quiet feeling, when manifesting my daily doings. I had a feeling like I had been a car without the head-lights, before the exploration of the "pure perceptions".

To call forth the "pure perceptions" aka meditation, I used to stop my thoughts, giving it an impossible task, because the brain of a nowaday person doesn`t work on full power. To force it to stop is kinda like making a restart to a computer.

For this, I gave it a tasks like "what was before nothing, before the light or the darkness, before there was no matter nor vacuum, the time nor space?"

With this question, my thoughts were overwhelmed and silenced, like a schoolboy on the attention, and the *pure perception* kicked in. A perception that knew, felt and created the answer.

One day a man came to visit my father. That man was known as someone who saw the aura colors of a human being and knew how to find sources of water in the ground with twigs. Of course it meant, that I was there to ask him questions.

He showed me how he not only finds the water, but how one can *gauge* energy fields of the fellow humans, trees and plants with those *magic twigs*. He also said what kind of aura colors he can see and told me to try it.

To one of my statements: "I don`t know, I think I can`t see them" he answered: "Sure you can."

Well, that was decided then.

Later I began to try that *gauging* to find a water from the ground, with the same *magic tools* he used. He used some copper wire, that he found on the ground, saying that it`s all the same—the twigs, the wires—only your friendship with a tool counts and the matter of tuning yourself.

For a half an hour, I almost strained my energies with those stubborn wires, standing like a welder, the way that even the last supper came to watch. Still nothing.

"What in the heavens sunday are you doing?" my guardian angel Kathy had observed me silently and stepped closer.

"I don`t know . . . waiting for something to happen?" I said.

"Like what? A lightning?"

"No. I`m trying to find the water source. How am I doing?"

"Good," she said and smiled: "If you want to be a traffic sign."

"It`s not as easy as it looks."

"Well, actually . . . It looks like you do nothing. Is that difficult?" she laughed her joyful and compassionate laugh.

"You should know," I smiled to her. "So try to do something and help me out, will you?"

"Finally you asked!" she sighed with happiness.

"So," she started and went on, "what you are doing is based on a percepting the energy field. You do percieve well though, because of your improved vibraton and the energyflow, but the secret lies within those three subjects of doing: communication, expression and focusing.

"Communication?" I started from beginning.

"Communication is a foundation of the motion of the energy, diffusion of the force. Represent yourself to the Allness and to your *magic tool*."

I did as it was told.

I felt a nice warmness flowing into my body, just like the sun shining not only on me, but also into me.

"Second—express yourself energetically. It`s easier than it sounds. You do this all the time, just not the councious way. Let the relationship of your hand and your *magic wand* to be the energetic expression of your *will*. Do it in a Great Spirit."

"Like an artist with a brush?"

"Yes. Let the Great Spirit guide it energetically. This is a normal state for all humans—to be the expression of the Great Spirit through their own Creation of Soul."

"And now I focus? To what?" I asked and looked around me.

"To the energy. To the feeling. And the knowing. These are all the same in a pure perception. Just move inside the energies, inside an Energetic World, and let the brush do it`s work."

I focused on the knowing or imagination, what the water source in the ground might be energetically. I moved from one room to the other inside my house.

Then suddenly!

The instrument in my hand moved! It was just like a compass. It seemed as if that "friend" in my hand gained some kind of an electrical charge, that reacted to the energy in the center of the water sources. When I say "friend", it is because it seemed that it came to life in my hands.

I ran outside, to try to gauge the energy fields of the trees. I chose a cedar tree, planted by me, near the big old stones.

I focused on that tree, communicating with him, and the *magic tool* in my hand was pointing to the center of the energy-source—the cedar tree.

Around it, there was an energetic circle-area with a diameter of 4 meters—the energetic field of a cedar-tree.

"When being in that area of the energetic field, you are connected with the source of the energy," Kathy explained. "If he accepts you, he will give you, in the most loving way, all that you need, because you are a Child of God and you represented yourself as one, being cincere and being the incarnation of the Truth."

"This is the universal communication?"

"Yes. An energetic communication. That is why the plants and the stones and other things do not mumble like you," she laughed with her bluish aura of goodness.

"You said *the energetic field*. What is that exactly?" I asked, appreciating her jokes.

"Everything is energy. The energy is a source of the information, consisting of the Light and the Information. Just like the Light enchants and inspires, the energy emits an impulse of communication. If the particle of energy of the source wants to communicate, then the force of the motion is born, that aimes the Information outside from the source of the energy and the Light—that in it`s nature is a communication—carries the Information safely and harmonically from the energy source to outside, in all directions. That is how an energetic field is created."

For some time after, I tried to *gauge* the energetic fields of a various people. It was a warm day of a beautiful autumn, when me and my brother were standing on a bridge of the nearest town, where a lot of people were passing by.

My brother is one year older than me and we do these cool things together and talk about the spiritual subjects.

As I was holding the *magic tool* in my hand, I turned my back to the passing citizens, so they wouldn`t think that we were the Ghost Busters.

The usual radius of the people`s energetic field was 2 to 5 meters. Some of the spiritual healers` energetic field is a lot bigger, hundreds of meters even.

With my brother, we *gauged* various things. The thrill and fun was limitless, when we realized that with this *magic tool*, we can *gauge* the qualities of another persons, concentrating on how much someone has joy or stupidity, sense of humor or selfishness, wealth or long age—for everything the *magic tool* gave an answer in the form of the radius that we compared with the others.

Also I could determine the north and the south with this newly found friend.

And of course the vibration of the books, which helped me to choose, what was worth reading and what`s not, without having actually to read it.

"The thing is," my guardian angel stated, "that everything has a vibration of it`s Creator. If you have a high level of vibration and purity, you can write about anything, even shoe-sizes and you still bring a lot of Light into the

World, bringing your readers closer to the level that you are vibrating on."

There you go.

Then this wonderful tool helped me to *read* the energetic value of a food. The greatest energy field is the food that is grown by a loving person, in one`s Living Engrained Home. And the food that was bought from the store, the greatest energetic field had the honey, the nuts and eggs, with a diameter almost 2 meters.

Then there is an energy field of the gifts. The warmest gifts, that come from the heart, has an energetic field, with the radius of several meters. Sometimes even more than some people have.

But the interesting thing is, that the gift`s energetic field is similar to the one who gave it to you. These gifts can be protective talismans and heal the owner.

One day I realized—all the energetic beings had an energy field. I tried to *gauge* my guardian angel`s energy field and the *magic tool* worked perfectly. Although her energy was a lot more lighter and softer then a human being`s or food`s or bugs and animals, the *magic friend* showed the exact point where Kathy was standing in the room. I even tried to detect ghosts. That was fun. Not recommended for the fainted-hearts.

The another amazing topic was the energetic field of the water.

In the area of my home village, there is a powerful healing spring that is called The Fountain of the Sight. The water from that spring has an enormous energetic field.

I tried to recreate that water with my *will*, with the help of the Angels, to bring a Divine Energy into my water, and I was successful. This water can cure any disease and it has been successful in my years of healing people.

"The *gauging* the energetic field is a nice trick," Kathy said one day, "but the importance lies in the existence of an energetic field. It is important to know, that every energy source, whether organic or inorganic, is affected by your energy and vibration. Your state of being is responsible, whether the materia that is surrounding you inside your energetic field, is reviveing or destructing. That is why it is sacredly important, that a warrior-angel is a tuned on a high-vibrations in every second of his or her life, because their energetic field is very large and creates the world in massive radius. If I could send all the people in the world a message, then I wish that they knew, that their state of being has an unending importance to the Allness around them and that the simple state of Love as the Blessing Bluish Light would be enough."

THE BLESSING BLUISH LIGHT

The winter came with the sudden frost that year.

In this bright cold night, the Moon and the stars were shining allseeingly over the hybernated land.

I was lying again in the soft, white and sacredly shining snowdrift, thinking the warm thoughts about my dreams and about my wonderful life in this amazing world.

"I miss seeing everything from up there just like these stars do," I said to myself not knowing where this longing came from. I had a feeling that I used to do it, only that I didn`t have any memories about that action.

On that night I fell asleep in my hermit`s forest-house, with a warm wish to see the world. Leaving my body to the warm embrace of a soft duvet, I transmitted my energy particles and the perception matrix to the Allness . . .

Being wandering flowingly out of the time and space, in the dream worlds, I suddenly gathered myself together as my Higher Self, as the ray of soul, on the edge of our solar system.

I saw, how I was passing by from the planets, which were similar to the descriptions that I've heared in school about them. Rather, it felt like the planets were passing by me instead, and I was the one who stood still.

With a blink moment, I was on the border of the atmosphere of the planet Earth, seeing the oceans and the continents and had a very up close view of the Moon.

With an instant I flew even closer to the Earth, viewing it`s bluish glow embracing the globe. Transferring myself closer and closer, I saw a bright white bluish dots, that emanated the same light that surrounded the Earth. I felt a overwhelming grace and love.

Suddenly something started to supress my attention, just like a noise or anguish. An enourmous amount of red dots appeared, which were located on the parts of the most populated areas. I determined, that in those places should be the big cities.

I tried to focus on the bright spots, to find an explanation to what I was seeing. Though the bluish bright dots were located more dispersed and were less numbered, the area of the aura of those dots was greater, which the blusish ringing glow embraced. The very big bright bluish spots were located in Australia, India and Siberia, plus a lot of smaller ones all over the planet. There were thousands of them.

I couldn`t concentrate further, and fell into my body in the bed and blinked my eyes.

The next day, admirering the glow of a dancing flame of the candle, I was thinking about what I saw at night. Behind the window, the big majestetic snowflakes were falling.

Kathy was suddenly beside me, sitting on the table.

With taking a sip from a hot, relaxing tea of a rose hip, I asked Kathy:

"Want some tea?"

"Maybe later. A lot later," she blinked her eye to me.

"Ok. I wanted to ask from you, about what I saw that night. As I understand, the human being emanates the Light of some sort, was that it?"

Kathy tried to act as if she tangles her feet, sitting on a table:

"Yes. The Human Being emanates a very special kind of the Light in the Universe. This Light is visible and can be represented in all the Levels of Being."

"But I saw the two different types of Light, I saw colors."

"You did. Every Human Being can emanate various specters of that Light. The specter of being is one's free choice."

I recollected, how one of the Light specters was warm and inspirering, the other one was unpleasant to concentrate on.

"Kathy, some of the people emanated the same Light that the planet Earth was emanating."

"Our sincerely loved Creator, our Dad, emanated in the time of Dreaming—creating the world—the same Blessing Bluish Light. That Light gave a life to everything and gives it still, because He holds His loving *ray of soul* close to the planet Earth.

A Human Being—His Child—is like Him, and is able to emanate the same Light, if that is one's *will*."

"I saw these dots of Blessing Bluish Light around the world. Were these the people who emanate the same Light that our Dad does?"

I poured myself another cup of warm tea with the heavenly unique aroma.

"The Light was His, but they were not single persons, they were a communities of people, you didn't glimpse close enough to see the Light of a one person. In these groups and communities, that emanated The Blessing Bluish Light, lived happy people, who's love, the way of life or the causes were at a high level.

The red dots you saw, were a communities, in which the people generally on their Plain of Emotions, felt the same feelings that you did when concentrated on them—the anguish, the oppressiveness and depressing noise. It is a highly important for the Allness, that from the planet Earth, in general, the Blessing Bluish Light would emanate."

"Compared to these red dots, the bright one's were outnumbered—these blissful communities."

"They are not outnumbered at all. Even one of these loveful happy communities is more powerful than 1000 reds at the same size. And anyways, did you think you came here to just drink tea?" Kathy smiled. "You wanted to come here to help. And puff—here you are."

"I should make all people more happy? That they would be loved and their way of life would be exemplary, and that their Causes were at a high level?"

"Start with one person," she said. "It's a good start."

"With what can I begin to help someone to emanate The Blessing Bluish Light?"

"With trying," she looked up somewhere into the Heaven and smiled.

THE CODE OF A
WARRIOR-ANGEL

"There is a code for us," my guardian angel Kathy stated, sitting on the big rock on the side of a forest.

"A code of a warrior-angel."

"A code? I have to act by the code now?" I asked with a smile, lying on the grass and looking into the blue warm sky with the artistic marshmellowy clouds.

Her teachings just kept coming like the bills.

"First of all—acting is a very creative state of being. So you should definately be creative. Creative through the honor of your Soul. And you already brought up the first gift of the code—you don`t have to do anything."

"I don`t have to do anything?"

By asking this question, I suddenly felt the limits and restraints flew into the sky, leaving me as a still lake or a clean slate of an artist`s book. The school, the position in the society, just vanished like a bad mood on a picnic.

Everything I thought I had to do, just set me free, like there was no clocks or calendars in the world. It was here and now. I felt a few pounds lighter.

"The first gift of the code will give you the freedom you have as a warrior-angel. When you deeply percieve it, you will find that you are free to change anything in the Universe. Everyone is. Just like our Invisible Dad was, when He dreamed all this."

"I feel you," I told Kathy. "When I thought myself free like this, I had a feeling it is up to me in this moment, to choose between what feels right and what feels wrong. Between the good and evil. I am not only feeling that my moments are entirely up to me, but also the fate of the world. Is that possible?"

"It is. The first gift of the code will give you the power of the Free Will. So the next time you need to make changes in the world, when you are in a position where you can help someone, you are able to choose to do so. The restraints of the Dark Forces will not bind you to stop. You are able to perform miracles, just like Jesus chose to do it with his free will, and our Dad chose freely to bring joy through his gift of the Free Will."

"I will think this through," I uttered.

"The second gift of the code of a warrior angel, is the Honor and Acceptance."

"The Honor and Acceptance," I repeated, so I could remember it.

"This means," Kathy explained, "that you should honor everything and everyone around you through accepting the way things are. Accepting that everything and everyone are originated from a Free Will that is equal to yours. You should never control anything but your choises. The energies will follow to the Free Will. The gift of the Honor and Acceptance will give you a harmonic way to use the creative power through the Live Lead Example. That is how our Invisible Dad uses His power and that is the only effective way to change something better. What you do in life, goes into the Eternity."

I was amazed. I breathed deeply.

"The third gift of the code of a warrior-angel is the Sharing of the Light. Do you want to repeat it?" my guardian angel smiled kindly.

"The Sharing of the Light," I repeated joyfully.

"It means, that a warrior-angel always shares his Light, in every form, in every second of his incarnation. When you embrace these gifts of the code, you will always have a Light to share, whether less of it or plenty. In the form of a kind words, abundance you have to share, knowledge, love or a still heart—you should always share it with someone, whether it is a person, animal, the nature, the Universe or the God. You are there to share everything good that you have. To share it with the outside.

If you don`t have enough Light to give, then you should Create it, to give it away for the happiness of your surroundings. It`s like the love for your children—you give anything for their happiness. Embracing the gift of Sharing the Light, will bring you in the position of our Father, and that will bring forth the Divine Power, that our Dad has, and maybe the Energy of Love will help you on every step of your divine creation of this incarnation as a Child of God."

"Kathy, this is so beautiful . . ." I was weeping tears, because of the force of understanding in my heart and soul. Or maybe it was the recognition.

"And finally—you should know that a warrior-angel is not a title. It is a way of percieving yourself. It brings us closer to the point of our birth and the origin. To our home in the Beyond. It gives you the power to understand yourself, to recognize. All human beings have the same power of Creation. A warrior-angel uses this power to harmonize the surroundings. To watch over it.

A warrior-angel makes a little paradise—a Living Engrained Home—for the Energy of Love to have an atmosphere to stay in, so that the most Lightful energy would aid and support the warrior-angel in all his quests. This imitation of the Garden of Eden will caress and embrace the warrior-angel and gives him the powers of a Human Being. The natural abilities of the Child of God.

A warrior-angel lives healthy, feeding on the goods that is being growed in his Living Engrained Home and drinks the revitalizing water from the area near the place of his Living Engrained Home.

He wakes up in the morning, being thankful for every Light he has to give on that day, breathing the sweet air of his ecological garden that he created, and thinks about what he will do for other people on that day to make them happy and loved.

In this safe and natural environment, the Energy of Love will float, calling the soulmate to the greatest creation in the Allness—a birth of a new pure Human Being. Through the century of love—their life—he and she will shine a Light of the Live Example, for their divine children and make the most precious gift for the generations to come—a gift, which is the incarnation of love that is the Loving Home in the garden of paradise, created together with the God and the soulmate.

The happy cheering children will run barefeet to your arms wide open, when you and your soulmate laugh in love, in the wonder of the gift of a life and the blessing to bequeath the wonderfully beautiful world to the children of Light, that you brought into this world by being worthy to aim the Light of Allness through the state of love, through your every glimpse of the everlasting incarnations."

THE LIVING ENGRAINED HOME

"Kathy! Will you talk to me, please?" I said to my guardian angel on a clowdy warm summer day, sitting on a bench under the birch tree. She appeared to my right, sitting happily and smiling.

"That was fast, wasn`t it?" she laughed.

"Yeah. You travel fast. And light. I wanted to ask you something."

"Then I will try to answer," she was wellwishingly kind.

"Why a Living Engrained Home? I know it`s a place, similar to the Garden of Eden, a paradise on Earth, but isn`t the nature enough?"

"The Living Engrained Home is not just a pure nature and the garden to be. It is a place that will keep you going. Your body, soul and spirit. It is very important, that a warrior-angel would have a solid ground to stand on, when fighting a good fight."

"How so? I thought the power of a warrior-angel comes within?"

"That`s true. But you are now incarnated. That means, that you need to honor some rules of that planet.

To give others, you need to have something to give. Through-out a millions of years, the only constant abundance has been the Living Engrained Home. All the other values change in a blink of an eye, if you look down on Earth through the various Eras. Everything changes. Every value of a certain abundance depends on the Image that is created on that period of time.

It only takes a minor change, and the illusore value of the valuables, food, positions in society, money, even countries, will change. The abundance is a normal state of a Human Being, which our Eternal Dad wanted for His Children. He gave the nature with delicious fruits, seeds and vegetables to keep the "food on the table" for every Godly Human Being, who will be born in this paradise. In the time of the Living Engrained Homes, people honored this abundance by creating their homes in a harmony with His Dream, understanding it`s importance.

They knew that the Living Engrained Home, embraced by the Atmosphere of the Energy of Love, will not only keep the body healthy and strong, but also gives abundance to the soul and the spirit, giving them sufficient energy to accomplish anything and everyone in that paradise would have a connection with the Cosmos and with all the information in the Universe. They could also communicate with the thoughts of the God.

The downcome, the need, famines and sicknesses came, when people started to leave their Living Engrained Homes, forgetting the knowledge of their ancestors.

A warrior-angel should have a Living Engrained Home, not to be dependent on such changes in the society, so a warrior-angel itself would be able to give.

A warrior-angel is always able to give Light in every form, because the giving is a warrior-angel`s natural state of being.

A warrior-angel keeps the body, mind and spirit on the highest level possible, and then evolving further, to be better in helping others. The Living Engrained Home is a major part of that balance."

"So the life is like a tree and the Living Engrained Home is like the land?"

"Exactly," Kathy nodded. "Every stone, a plant and a flower will send the owner of the Living Engrained Home a constant energy, joy and protection. That is when the owner of the Living Engrained Home is worthy of their friendship and the affection.

When the link between the ancestral knowledge—the Primeval Wisdom—was cut by the Dark Forces, people lost their Image of the Living Engrained Home, with the honor and divinity to understand it`s purpous.

That is why a lot of people still have the gardens, where they grow food, but they don`t really have the affection of the nature.

The Atmosphere of the Energy of Love has to be present, or the nature will not name you it`s worthy ruler."

"How could we get back the Primeval Wisdom?"

"By communicating with our Dad through our feelings and surroundings. That is where the people of the Era of the Living Engrained Home got their wisdom to harmonize the world, living in the atmosphere of the Energy of Love.

They tried to learn every thought of the God, through their own Living Engrained Home. Every bit of His wisdom is still present in the details and the connections of His Creation—the nature. When you fully understand the surroundings—every animal, a plant, a stone and a drop of the wonderful rain—the world around you will name you a worthy ruler, a God or a Goddess.

That is how the fellow people called the owners of the Living Engrained Homes on the times of old, because of their ability to create harmony, similar to His.

Some of the Living Engrained Homes lasted for tens of thousands of years, giving their owners a gift of the reincarnation again and again in the happy harmonic life with the abilities like using *the ray of soul*, talking with Him, the teleportation, the telekinesis, the telepathic abilities and the high speed of thoughts, that made them possible to manifest anything through the Living Images. Today, there is a way to get these normal abilities back, through the miracle of the Living Engrained Home."

"And I can create this Living Engrained Home for myself and for my soulmate and for our children?" I was very affected by this thought.

"Of course. Everyone can. All you need is a little land and a dream to live close to Him with your soulmate and with your divine children, through the Atmosphere of the Energy of Love. But before you do anything, try to build the Living Engrained Home in your mind, with all the details, and try to understand His harmony and Thoughts of the Creation."

"I`m gonna start right now to dream that paradise," I was so inspired to Create something similar with God.

"Good. Because every harmonic Living Engrained Home will give balance to the whole World. Good luck, my dear warrior-angel!" she said and smiled.

THE LINES OF TIMES

"Kathy, you say often the words "nowadays humans". What was the people like before?" I asked from my guardian angel.

"In which time?" she answered cheerfully.

"I don`t know. What kinds of times are there?"

"Well, the Mankind has repeated the same pattern for billions of years. In some times, the humanity has been happy and harmonic, the other times their choices brought the way of life into the brink of an abyss."

"Tell me about the times of harmony. Maybe that is what we should be concentrated on, to improve our way of life. Tell me about the times of the Living Engrained Homes."

"Good," my guardian angel said. "I think it`s important to connect The Lines of Times."

"The Lines of Times?"

"It was someone`s intentions, to cut The Lines of Times, so the Mankind didn`t know the wiseness of the past. It was like cutting the tree from it`s roots, spraying some water on the leaves for a price of that *unimaginable* mercy. That is how they wanted to rule everything. In the times of harmony, on the other hand, all people lived connected with The Lines of Times."

"Can someone rebind The Lines of Times?"

"Every person can do it. I will show you how," Kathy told me.

"Thank you."

"Sit tight," she said. "The Lines of Times are inside you, I will try to rebind some of them, using the words."

The next thing I remember, it was like some kind of a trance, an awe. Induced by her words. Like a dream that I saw, which I couldn`t wake up from, but I still had a feeling in my arms and legs and body. Like the pictures running through my mind, which I couldn`t take my concentration off. They just kept flowing with a surge of energy.

The first and the last words I remember Kathy said, were:

"It was the time, when the sky was more etheral. The atmosphere was glowing brighter because of the Energy of Love from the Living Engrained Homes. One of these paradisely gardens was at the south side of a slow river. The house of that Living Engrained Home was carved carefully from the cedar trees. Look!

Under that apple tree, behind the house, is sitting a young girl. She has a long brown hair and a graceful but strong sporty body, with white linen dress. It`s her birthday today, that is why the garden is so dedicated to her, with the Light of the Cosmos. They called her Shenna . . ."

. . . She had three yellow apples in her hands. She caressed them softly, putting the warmth of her Soul into them, as she whispered in the heat of her dream:

"Dear Invisible Dad," she turned to the God.

"Dear Invisible Mom," she smiled to the Energy of Love.

"*I am your visible daughter. At this time of the Lining, when the planets are nearest to the birth of the creation of mine, I only wish to bring Heaven into the world to be visible for all. I wish these apples to bring my soulmate to me, to whole the two Sacred Halves into One.*

I am a goddess, who carries the Light, burning to create and to share. I only want to shine for him, for my chosen one. For the one, whom I created this old garden with, centuries ago. Dear Mom and Dad—I hope I`ll bring you the eternal warmness of joy through my dream!"

It was the Day of the Rafts. It was customed on that day, to put the fruits of a Living Engrained Home on the raft, sending them on a mission to find the love for the century—the soulmate with whom to share the Great Creation with—the Atmosphere of Love in the Living Engrained Home. These rafts were led by a Divine Destiny and the power of the ray of soul, to the soulmate who was somewhere in the world. People of that time had the ability to sense where the fruits are from, when tasted, so these apples led the two Halves together.

The Day of the Rafts were usually for middle-age women, who hadn`t found their soulmate yet, so they readied themselves for the reunion of two, by improving themselves and in the Living Engrained Home of their parents, they grew the food with their Soul-print to put them on the rafts. The young people usually found their soulmates on the festivals of the nearby villages.

The young Shenna hadn`t found her soulmate. She sensed him to be somewhere else and that she will not find him on the festivals.

She sensed him better, because she was born in the Living Engrained Home, planted lives ago with him, with her soulmate.

She had taken care of this garden for 17 years. Her mother, who happened to be her great-great-great-grand-daughter, helped her with it, and so did her father and brother.

She had grown the apples for three months, talking with the tree and warming it with her ray of soul, so the fruits would be ready for the Day of the Rafts.

Suddenly her young brother appeared from the far side of the forest. He had brown hair and a long linen bright shirt and pants and the linen belt with the ebroidered epistel as the heirloom of the family.

He was a quick runner, as he jumped over the fences of the Living Engrained Home, that were made from the thick bushes. He ran towards Shenna and stopped 20 yards away from her. It was not appropriate to interrupt the Child of God from thinking.

Shenna nodded her head and her brother got a permission to enter into her space.

"What is it, Adin?" she asked form her out-of-breath brother.

"The bear. He needs our help!"

Shenna put her apples in the scarf and said:

"Lead the way."

They ran to the forest, uphill, and found their bear, who helped them in the household, hanging on the tree that was bended across the ravine of that slow river.

"I climbed on a tree, to bend it over the ravine to cross it. Mumzy tried that too, but he was too heavy," Adin said. "Can you push him with your ray of soul?"

"No," Shenna answered. "I can`t visualize myself to the air and have a ground to push from. I haven`t listened that topic through yet. The Elders still teaching us to calculate the Live Images with the ray of soul, in the Cirlce of Stories."

"If we could bend another tree to Mumzy, that could lift him . . ." Adin suggested.

"*I have to calculate,*" *was the words of Shenna, as she took a meditation position.*

After a blink while, she opened her eyes and said:

"*That one.*"

She was pointing on a long aspen tree, that was longer than the spruce tree under it.

"*I saw that if we both climb up to that tree, it will bend down exactly there,*" *she was pointing at the bear,* "*and when Mumzy grabs it, the strong spruce next to the aspen tree holds it steady until we climb off, and then leaver of these two trees that Mumzy holds on, will lift him up.*"

"*Let`s go then,*" *Adin said and started running towards the aspen tree. He saw that Shenna didn`t follow and stopped, asking:*

"*What is it?*"

"*I also saw that I will lose my apples,*" *she uttered, looking the scarf with three apples.*

"*How?*"

"*I didn`t see.*"

"*Leave them here.*"

"*I know,*" *she said.* "*But it may not be enough . . .*"

The tree where the bear was hanging, made a cracking sound.

Shenna put the scarf near the roots of another tree, the far away as possible, and they climbed up to the aspen tree.

Everything happened exactly like Shenna had calculated with the Living Images. Except the detail, when the bear was rising up with a speed, after he was on the top, he leaned on the other way with his weight, landing on a smaller tree behind the aspen and the spruce, which bended so hard that it`s roots came out from the ground. Under that tree, the scarf with the apples was, and the roots hit them right into the abyss of that ravine.

Shenna breathed deeply and calmly, though the sadness was seen in the gesture of her hands. Adin understood what she had done, what she had sacrificed.

He made a little bow to her for the sign of gratitude and honor.

Shenna did the same and her brother went to hug the bear and to calm him.

Shenna had lost the opportunity to be a part of the Day of the Rafts.

She went and picked up a red scarf and dried a tear with it, sitting down slowly.

She sat there a while, thinking she may have to wait for another year to find her love, when suddenly she heared a ringing tone in her ears. The people of that Era knew, that it was the sound of the Bright Forces.

She got up with a heroine move and went towards Adin and Mumzy. She stopped a bit away from them. Adin smiled to her and made a gesture with the hand, saying it is ok to interrupt them.

Shenna said:

"Can you both do something for me?"

Mumzy joyfully got up and shaked himself like being ready.

"Of course," Adin smiled. "What can we help you with, dear sister?"

"This tree will not grow anymore," she pointed on a tree with the roots out of the ground. "I need you to build me a raft. A bigger one. A big enough to carry me. I may not have the apples, but I have the Energy of Love."

My vision started to haze. Everything went black for a while and I saw my surroundings.

"Can I go back?" I asked from Kathy.

"Of course. The only thing you need to do is to rebind the Lines of Times. Then you are able to recollect anything from the past of your ancestors and from their future."

"Good. I`d like to see how the story ends."

"It will never truly end . . ." my guardian angel smiled and vanished to go do some errands.

THE SIGNS

I re-entered into the vision of that Era, trying to find out more about the people of another time.

I tried to focus on the details of what I saw, until they started to flow by themselves, pulling me into the trance again . . .

Shenna, Adin and Mumzy pushed the raft into the river. The other women on the shore looked silently at them with the surprised smiles. With honor they sighed.

"Adin. Mumzy. Thank you," Shenna bowed.

"Let the Divine Quest of your Soul bring the Light of Love into this world," Adin said and gave her a bag with the food from their Living Engrained Home.

Mumzy padded on the raft two times with his paw, making sure it holds his mistress.

"I'll be back soon," she said to the bear, letting him to push the raft on it`s way. Through the three big stones, the raft started to move patiently towards the destiny.

Hours went by.

Shenna heared a bump through her dreaming. The ancient morning fog carpeted the old pure nature. The raft had carried her the whole night, until eventually some branches and a stone caught the journeyness into it`s end.

The raft was stuck.

Just like the other people of that Era, Shenna was able to "collect The Signs."

These signs were known as the Beacons of the Destiny, showing a harbor to the mission of the present incarnation—the Divine Plan.

One of the branches was stuck, pointing towards the little yellow single flower, floating like it was alive—dancing. It was The Sign.

Shenna got off from the raft, trying to percieve the Message of the Sign. She couldn`t determine one.

She breathed deeply and smelled the scent of that yellow golden flower, on a swampy shore of a quiet river.

Suddenly, from the point where she was standing, she saw a yellow-golden glowing flower on a distance, under the mossy old tree, through the spot where the fog was vanished, creating something like a hazy tunnel. It was the same flower that the branch was pointing at and it was somehow blinking through the thick fog.

"The Continuum," she whispered.

The people of old called the Waves of the Signs, with the meaningfulness—Continuum.

She went to the yellowish fresh cold flower, trying not to step into the water-moss.

Behind that bended old tree, the mysteriousness of that old forest revealed the fair animal path. Well-rested Shenna looked around her, seeing how the early birds flew to admire her with the interested notes of their sky-songs.

She took the path, until the thicket stopped her from continueing the road.

She sat on the roots of a tree to explore her options.

She considered whether or not to fly up with the ray of soul to scout the forest for direction.

Shenna suddenly looked behind her. She had heared a sound of a wooden door.

"That's odd," she was thinking by herself, standing up slowly and searched for a source of that noise.

"Where is the house of that door?"

She felt the rich light aromas of the morning chilly forest, from the direction where the sound reappeared again.

Suddenly she was experiencing something like a dizzyness and the next step she took, seemed to land 10 yards to the right, from where she was standing.

Shenna had stepped into the Living Engrained Home garden with an old house.

She hesitated for a while, whether or not to go and knock on the door.

The atmosphere of that Living Engrained Home accepted her and she felt warmness in her soul. Something in that atmosphere liked her.

Before she could push aside the long straws of the raspberries, to go knock on that strange door, she saw someone standing on the threshold of that mysterious house, raising his hand to greet the stranger.

Everything was so familiar to her, almost like she had lived there once. The old oak tree on the west side of the house, the pile of stones under the forest line on the north and the wonderful little golden-yellow and white flowers with the round leaves.

"Why did I turned up to be here?" Shenna thought and breathed. "Maybe the closeness of that house was because of my soulmate who lives here?"

Smilingly and gracefully, with her eyes lowered, she went to greet the young man on the door.

Closer and closer, until raising her eyes to look him in the eye.

"It`s not him," she stopped, thinking by herself.

"I greet you, goddess of the Earth," the young man bowed.

"I do it gladly also, kind Creator of this amazing garden," Shenna answered, lifting her beautiful hair behind the ear.

The people of that time knew intuitively clear, whether the other person is their soulmate or somebody else`s.

"I am Kado. I didn`t create this garden alone. But you must be very similar to him, if you found the pass into our home. Sorry about him, he likes to joke like this."

"Who?" Shenna asked, raising the hand so a little curious bird could land on it.

"My brother. Oh, and he likes to sleep a lot, that is why he is so good with his ray of soul. He is doing it right now."

They heared something was falling in the house. Seemed like something cracked and smashed and Kado made the gesture with his eyes, like knowing which housware he will never see again.

Someone was wowing in the house.

Shenna giggled smoothly, raising her shoulders a bit.

"Kado, it worked!" they heared from the house.

"I managed to transfer my body to the ray of soul. I found some apples by the river and . . ."

They heared the voice came closer: " . . . I was looking at these apples with my ray of soul and suddenly something pulled my body and I woke up there on the side of a river and . . ."

Shenna saw him.

He had a thick short brown hair and a strong vital body. He also had green eyes and a well-wishing smile.

The cheering young man looked into her eyes, forgetting to bow to a goddess, who could figure out his mental barriers around the house.

"Shenna," she told her name to introduce herself, through the lightful burst of the warm feelings she tried to restrain.

"Darden," he answered honorably, almost not able to catch his racing feelings.

"They are yours, aren`t they?" Darden reached his hands towards her with the three apples and continued:

"I tried to find their raft, but I couldn`t. Here. Take them. If you want to sail them down the river to find what you are waiting for."

But unheardably he said that he would like to keep them forever.

"They are yours. Keep them," Shenna said. "I already found you."

Darden went to her, standing close, gazing silently into her eyes. His brother went inside the house, without a word.

Darden touched Shenna`s hand and she fell into his warm embrace.

There is no words to express how long they stood there, in each-other`s kindly waiting hands, for the time was relative in the recognition of the Two Sacred Halves.

"I know these apples," Darden said.

"They are from our garden. From our Living Engrained Home. Of course YOU were the one to find them . . . Of course . . . But when did you recognize my soul-print in them?"

"Right away," Darden smiled and continued: "I was going to find you, using the apples. But suddenly there you were. On my doorstep."

Darden took her both hands and pressed them to his chest, close to his heart, saying:

"Come with me, dear Goddess of the Universe. I call you to the Great Creation. Will you be my inspiration, to create the Light and Eternity through our old Living Engrained Home?"

"I will go with you, my love. My soul is bright and ringing to Create with you, my dearest. Let our Living Engrained Home bring joy and Light to everyone once again and let the

Energy of Love live around us forever, through our peaceful dreams together."

With every second full of harmony, they went and lived many times through their divine Living Engrained Home.

Finding each-other again and again in the paradisley harmony and endlessness of the Lightful Dream of our forever-loved Father.

THE AWAKENING

"Oh, what a beautiful morning!" I said on one of my 23-rd springs on this Earth. It had been almost 10 years from the first time I spoke with my guardian angel.

I could say, that a gorgeus life embraced me through the peace and clarity.

I had fixed an enourmous amount of small details in my life, that binded me, exhausted and knitted a webs of illusions like an invisible spiders, trying to catch me.

I had enough of the spiders, I finally felt that I can rise by the beautiful rainbows of fate.

In me, there was fixated a wish to really start helping the world.

I had achived a level that high, that I started to love being me. I really adored it.

I felt so good as being myself and I knew, how I emanated the bliss, that filled my surroundings and made it ring.

I loved so deeply to be in the aureol of that bliss, to fly in the invisible hights and just BE.

I felt and knew, that I was emanating the Blessing Bluish Light, and with that I could empower everyone who I meet with.

I felt, that it is time for me to step into the world. It was time to meet my soulmate.

At last, I was completely ready to look her into her eyes and all else was just a backround music.

It is very important to know that not the one you love will bring you the happiness, but that the happiness must come from yourself and your happiness is to give it to your soulmate. To multiply the happiness you emanate.

I felt that at last I have something worth shareing—the Blessing Bluish Light. And that this could be enough.

I haven`t talked for months with my guardian angel. I had no need for that.

I solved a wonderous mysteries inside of me, opened up the new knowledge and explored the Allness that was in me.

I lived in a state of bliss.

"I`m ready," I whispered to the Everlasting Dad. "I am able to make your daughter, a Goddess of a Universe, happy. The one who is my soulmate."

It was a warm day in May, the Sun was playing in the sky with it`s rays and the young greenness was lovingly stretching towards the Light.

I was so happy saying that.

I didn`t know what was coming, but I felt that it was something amazing.

I was standing on the plot of my future Living Engrained Home. I had a piece of a cedar tree, with a string, in my hands.

I made the ritual to embrace it into my energetic field. I was standing on the grass with my bare feet, embracing the thing to my chest with my left hand, near the heart chakra. I felt the warm waves of the Light or rays floating through my body, when the Light of a cedar piece emerged with my Blessing Bluish Light.

The piece of a cedar tree will help to grant wishes by enhancing the Blessing Bluish Light of a bearer. The wish of the owner of that Light is honored in the Allness.

"My dear soulmate, my love . . . I wait and search for you. Please wait for me too, my dear . . ." I whispered, and caressed the little cedar piece that was like a necklace with a linen string.

A few green months passed by.

The Heaven shined with a divine depths of a ringing Light that day.

Kathy stood in her room of Light, in the Beyond, with the rays of a soft warmth landing on the boy she had guarded for over a million of years.

He was sleeping in an Earthly bed, sweet rays of a bluish light orbing around him, until he wakes up.

A tunnel of Light, with a golden walls, just like filming her guarded one, was vortexing towards Meckron.

Kathy sighed with an eternal peace and stillness.

"An important day," the violet angel of the awakening appeared beside her.

They knew what was coming.

Kathy was silent.

"It seems you did it," the violet angel said.

"I helped," Kathy answered, without moving her lips. "He is a warrior-angel. He did it by himself. There was no doubt in the First Aureola, that he will. And she has already made her choice."

"I heared. All the Heaven is talking about Samia and Meckron. They will meet today. You know what that means."

"The Awakening," Kathy levitated movelessly and with a firm slowness, looking into the channel of Light above.

"23 years," she said. "23 years and he`s ready. Just like He said he would. He knows Meckron and Samia well. All the efforts that we made . . ."

The violet angel nodded once.

" . . . it will bear fruit from now until forever," the violet angel ended her sentence.

Meckron moved. The Light around him started to flow. He started to wake up.

"Keep a watch," Kathy said to the other guardian angel of his and pointed the tunnel of Light to Samia. In her city apartment, she already was combing her beautiful thick brown hair, thinking about the oncoming day, when she will meet that boy from that spiritual forum in the internet.

She was a bit nervous, when spraying a serum on her hair.

Kathy smiled, seeing her, thinking how many years she wanted to tell Meckron about his Sacred Half, the one he was destined to meet—about Samia. But a guardian angel can not intervene like that.

Kathy aimed her ray of soul to Samia, to calm her. Samia felt the lightfulness in her happy heart.

"Finally I will meet him," her heart was filled with the anticipation. She went to pray, blessing the day and thanking for the opportunity, that her spiritual teachet gave her—a 70-mile ride to meet that special boy who Samia already held dear, through the midnight spiritual conversations they had.

Little did she know, how closely the Heavens were watching on that day. Though Samia was an angelic therapist to be, even with the wonderous psychic abilities she had, she couldn`t really know what will happen on that day or what a day of celebration it is in the Universe and the incarnations she had.

The Light fulfilled her rom on many levels, as her conviction was strong and heared in the Allness.

"I hope he likes me," she thought and grabbed her white blouse and it was time to go.

The Awakening of a Warrior-angel

Kathy saw how she left her apartment to start the journey. Kathy was there to make sure, that everything was according to The Plan.

It was a wonderful morning of July. On that morning, the peace overtook me. I knew, that today I will see Samia the first time.

I left from the forest house I lived in, stepping towards the incredible day with my bare feet on the morning damp cool grass.

"So. An important day, isn`t it?" I heared Kathy, who I haven`t spoke with for a long time.

"Well, well. And where have you been?"

"Everywhere with you. But you learned to handle yourself very good."

"Thanks, Kathy. That means a lot, coming from you."

I jumped over the web of a spider, accross the thin road, surrounded by a high straws of hay.

"You are almost performed an Awakening," Kathy continued.

"Almost?"

She smiled at my question, but didn`t answer.

Awakening—what does that mean? Do we wake up inside ourselves, seeing ourselves in the new point of view? Because we look at ourselves as another person who we have become? Then the awakening and hybernating comes hand-in-hand. If one part of us awakens—the present—then the other one is hybernating, and we call it the past.

Or does awakening means the activation of some of the parts of our being? What parts? When did they even hybernated? Why did they do that?

Can God perform an Awakening?

All the nature awakens and hybernates. A tree is a tree, always. We know that the tree awakens and hybernates. It`s a part of a tree. But what part of it? Maybe that part is a God in the tree?

Is the God an awakening and the hybernation, or is He in something, that is between them?

"The Light is between everything," I remembered a sentence from somewhere, as I was walking towards the moment to meet Samia.

I had a feeling that I was on the stage. I even had a sensation as seeing myself as I was a spectator. Was I an actor or a director? Or was I something that is between them?

I felt like I was going towards a happy ending. All that was in my life had brought me to this moment. To that point in the Universe.

I felt that I am the Light, between everything.

I waited. And waited. I waited for her.

Meckron was leaning on the car, thinking they will come at any second. Kathy saw how he was nervous.

"Just breathe," she heared him thinking, as the bright lightning of the energy sparked around him.

Kathy smiled. The green calming light came from above, the Light of an Archangel Raphael, landing on him. Meckron breathed deeply and calmly. Kathy saw a number of rays from the various First Aureols of the Heaven—a spectators of that sacred day.

Everyone was brightly anxious to see if they recognize each-other—the two Seraph from the nearest Ligt of His Presence, sent on Earth with a divine purpose.

Samia drove closer and closer. A bit more . . .

Just one curve . . .

There!

Samia saw a boy, leaning on a car.

"Who`s that boy?" one of her companions in a car, asked.

"That`s my husband," Samia heared herself thinking and her pounding heart was as loud as her thoughts for the Heaven.

Kathy laughed in tears, hearing Samia`s thoughts and the Allness held it`s breath.

The car stopped next to Meckron`s. He saw the driver, Samia`s spiritual teacher, but the other windows were toned, so he couldn`t see Samia.

"Follow me," he said to lead the way to the place he lived.

Meckron felt his heart racing and poundind. He could merely hold himself together.

Kathy knew, that he is feeling the same feelings as he did in his past lives, when the two Seraph met.

When they all finally got there and exited the cars, he saw her!

He saw Samia!

With her warm blue eyes and beautiful black hair, Samia exited the car into the bath of a dense sunlight.

She was so stunning and attractive, that it seemed the time had slowed itself at the arrival of her grace. She lowered her eyes and smiled to him. Meckron thought silently:

"So this is my Samia," and was startled because of that thought.

But loudly he said:

"Hello!"

Kathy saw on the energetic level, how the Lines of Times were creating and shifting, changing.

It happened when the two souls, who had planned their new meeting in the next life, met each-other.

A guardian angel Kathy saw their Lights merge at once, flowing like a slow vortex, like a dancing music. The rays of their kind light echoed their notes into the past and the future—everywhere at once.

All the present guardian angels saw—the energetic reality was changing, the waves of the Light were storming from them.

Kathy smiled and the other angels made a bow to her, for the special mission was over.

The Awakening had come to be.

As Samia and Meckron were spending their day together, meditationg, picking berries, walking on a warm July meadows, they felt the unbelievable happiness and the feeling of Home. Also from the Allness was seen, how they felt the heat and the sparking pull, like a gravitation of love, pulling them together like a magnets.

The long dress that Samia was wearing, fluttered slowly in the wind and her fresh scent filled Meckron`s mind and the atmoshere.

After a few hours, there was a time for a farewell.

Meckron didn`t feel like it was the goodbye.

He felt a new beginning.

He felt like home.

Just like he was up there again, in the Heaven, with his Dad and with the Energy of Love, vortexing into the Eternity of Creation with his twin-flame—his soulmate.

Samia looked into his eyes and raised her hand. He took it and they embraced each other, for hours as it seemed to the Allness and to them.

He loved her!

He felt what it means, when the time stops and only the love is in motion.

It seemed to him like he held her forever.

The Sun and the Moon and the stars were circling, but their love was constant.

Quiet.

Eternal.

She was his twin-flame—his soulmate.

They were whole again.

They were the two Sacred Halves.

They were the Light, between everything.

They were between the hybernation and the awakening.

They were between the Sun and the Moon. Between the Earth and Heaven.

Between the time and the timeless.

Between the two hearts.

Between the God and the Energy of Love. Between the incarnation and reincarnation.

They were as one!

Everything was between them and they were between everything.

They were the Divine Plan.

They were the Enlightment.

They were everything in everything.

And through that everything, they recognized each other.

He was her and she was him.

They were God.

They were awakened!

THE AFTERLIFE

"Well, that was different," I said out loud, when I was back in my body, in my bed, from a wonderous out-of-body experience.

My powers were growing immensly. It has been 2 weeks from the Awakening.

From the day I first met the love of my eternity.

From the day, when everything I ever dreamed of, came to me.

Samia still had some loose ends to tie up, in the city, until she could came to live with me, in the ancient nature of my birthplace.

I went to e-mail her about the night and what her *ray of soul* had showed me.

"My dearest Samia.

I was helping the two women with my ray of soul, who had stuck into the limbo. Just as I had pulled them out of that trap realm, so they could move on into the light, suddenly I saw you!

Out of no-where, a tunnel of a golden light opened up and you were gracely floating towards me from the Heavens.

You had a beautiful white-golden creamy aura around you and you looked like a goddess.

I understood—it was your Soul. You were a bit different, but I understood this was the way your soul looks like. I`ve never seen you so clear!

Just as you looked at me with your loveful eyes of the *ray of soul*, you started to speak.

But your language . . .

It was like a singing! The language of that Era was so melodical, so many feelings!

Today`s language sounds very monotone, compared to that.

You started a beautiful *song*, and every phrase you sang, was telling me more than a chapter from today`s book!

These phrases of your song, carried me into the slides and pictures of that time.

Then I understood—you wanted to show me our past. Our love. Our home.

I was floating higher than the clouds, with you by my side, my dear.

I saw the world. It had only one big ocean, and the other continents were as one, filled with the river rapids.

I realized—it was how the planet Earth looked like in that Era.

You took me closer to the ground. Closer and closer, until we saw a minor continent, surrounded by the massive rivers. It was located on south of the Atlantic Ocean, where there is an ocean right now.

In your *song*, you named that continent Tontorra. And you took me closer, showing me the land, filled with a thousands of villages.

You called this land with the name Daskia.

Closer and closer. Until we saw a beautiful house—a Living Engrained Home.

There was a wonderfully harmonic environment and a beautiful garden. Next to the carved wooden door, there was a gigantic flower, a giant bellflower, with a white-lilac tone.

Beside the house, an old tree was guarding the atmosphere of that Living Engrained Home, with a little wooden swing, tied to it`s branch.

Then suddenly you started to *sing* faster and longer phrases and I could see our whole life, running through my vision. How we met and how we grew some red berries, that were the size of a coconut, and how we gave these berries to the people who passed by our hand-made wooden fence of our Living Engrained Home.

And I saw how we raised our children, in our divine happy home, in the atmosphere of Love.

That language was too much to comprehend at once, so I remember only a bits of pieces of our life of the past, but I remember our love!

I felt just like this! How I feel about you right now!

My love! Inside me, there is now a million years of our live.

My goddess! My wife . . . My eternal Soulmate!"

"My love! Thank you!" she answered. "Thank you for remembering, my dear! For remembering me! For remembering us. For remembering our love!

I just can`t stop crying, I`m so happy . . . I`m so happy that I finally found you. My eternal love . . .

Thank you for being real!"

Our love was in the world again. Stronger. Brighter.

The love of a two seraph.

It was here to light up the world through the incarnation of us.

Through our eternal love and the link with the Higher Powers, we were here again. Again to help people to remember who they are and where they come from.

We were the two seraph, with a mission to help others to the Enlightenment and to bring the Heaven into this World by helping people to purify themselves and awaken their Soul to be closer with Him, with our Dad.

I realized, that I started to see the auras of the people. In every color, depending on their vibration.

When I went into the meditation, entering the Channel of the Angelic Energy, with my angelic form, I could see the energetic bonds around the people.

These energetic bonds were with a different colors and causes.

For instance, the red bonds with other people meant, that you are afraid or materially dependent of that other person. The blue ones, on the other hand, showed a bond of protection and a just communication.

I also found I could see the energetic stuff around people, during the Angelic Therapy Sessions, with which I helped people. Everything that is in the Universe, is seen on the energetic level.

As the negative affection part, there was seen the ghosts that drains the person, the demons, curses, the bad words, the holes in the aura and all kinds of disharmony.

During the Angelic Therapy Sessions, I cooperate with the Angels and we come with the Angels from the Highest Light, to that patient on the energetic level and purify the person from all the unnecessary energetic influence, so the person could go on with his Higher Path, heal from the chronic sicknesses or evolve further, having a better happy and harmonic life, without the restraints of the Dark Forces.

On the positive field, we could see the karmas and the visions on the Three Main Paths of the Life—the Path of the Spirituality, the Path of the Abundance and the Path of Love.

During the Angelic Therapy Sessions, we remove all the obstacles, that holds you down on these Paths, and miracles follow. We bring you to the right path—the one you have chosen before incarnating.

Also we could see the beautiful birth and the origin of the person`s Soul, the age and the type. We could see and communicate with the person`s guardian angels to mediate the messages from your angels, what you could do to improve your life in every field.

We could also see the magic beings and animals, who help the person and we help a person to communicate with them, to get a better cooperation with our invisible energetic friends and with the spiritual guides.

I went to visit Samia in the city.

It was a hot day of July.

I saw the guardian angels of the people around me, flashing all around them, like a spheres of a neon radiating light.

I saw beautiful Samia, with a linen white shirt and jeans, walking and emanating a bright tone all around her, as she was distinctive from everybody else.

She had a very large energetic field, so I felt her a half of a mile away and I had been walking towards her the last minutes.

There she was.

My wife from the ages ago.

I still felt the same way about her. For the woman I had only met once in this life. But I loved her and knew her like we have lived together for millions of years.

Our bodies were different again in this incarnation, so they were a bit shy. But we were the same. Just as I had seen in my vision that night, about our ancient life.

I looked into her kind an warm blue eyes.

Her look revived the incarnations we had and filled my soul with the Light of our Eternal Love.

We embraced each other.

The dark-blue thick roaming cloud brought the fresh rain, as we walked to her place, so I took her in my arms and we stood under the birch tree to find cover.

We were soaking wet and some of the drops may have been the happy tears, when we smiled in a pouring rain.

The Sun of our Eternal Invisible Dad came out again and dried us fast and carefully.

Later on, we went to the forest to meditate, holding each-other`s hand and the fairytaly flowers passed by us, like greeting the miracle of love.

During this meditation, I managed to go to the beyond, into the Heaven, to the place we are before incarnating.

I saw Samia right beside me and there was our Dad and the Energy of Love. I felt I was ringing with the happiness and the eternal joy.

Also there were a thousands of angels who had come to celebrate.

It reminded me a ceremony of a Sacred Marriage. Our Dad put a blessing light, that reminded me the crown and the tiara, on our heads and the angels sang their joyful gentle song.

After I returned to my body, I told Samia about it.

"I saw the same thing," she said. "I see the world differently now, do you?"

"The light," I pointed to the evening sun on the green tree-tops, "it`s different."

"I think it`s brighter. Like up there. And smoother," Samia said.

"Would you like me to swing you?" I asked her, referring to the swings on the area of sand, on the left. "I`d love to do it."

She nodded and gave me her smooth warm hand. I helped her up.

We went to the swings and as she sat there, my loving arms on her shoulders, I suddenly remembered!

I remembered a part of our previous life that she had showed me. In Daskia, when we first met.

We were little and I found her, swaying on a swing, waiting for someone to swing her.

I was watching her, wanting so much to be that person. So I just went and put my arms on her shoulders, without a word.

She was looking into my eyes with the look, that only she can give. Her ray of soul caressed me.

I smiled.

I touched the little girl`s wonderful neck and suddenly I kissed her slowly.

I touched her gorgeous perfect face and she kissed me back. And smiled.

I swing her slowly and we were silent.

The years of our love ran again like a pictures through my eyes, as I saw we had a swing in a garden of the house we lived in, to honor our first kiss and that we went there every time the stars and the moon were assembled the same, and I swinged her on a swing, kissing the passionate red lips and the loving eyes of my Eternal Wife.

I found myself, touching the gorgeous neck of hers, revealed by her dark vital long hair, that landed on her white top.

I kissed her suddenly, the first time in this life. I touched her shoulders and wonderful perfect face and she kissed me back.

The time stretched sacredly, as if it was a wonderful dream.

We both felt the lifetimes of love, what we have had.

There was only love in my life. A love fulfilled. And a back-ground music, played with the details of the beauty of the incarnation we had. Everything was so perfect and divine and untouchable.

"I remember us," I said. "I remember our lives together, my goddess," and I told her what I had remembered.

"I love you, my eternal soulmate," I whispered to her.

"I love you too, so much . . ." she smiled.

The happy tears of a Sacred Love between the two seraph, fulfilled our smiling eyes.

Our souls were singing.

The world stayed hazy with a bright soft light of the Heaven, as we floated on the forest road of a Fairytale.

Now and forever.

To where?

Into our lives together . . .

Into the Eternity . . .

Into the Heaven . . .

To save the World . . .

It wasn`t the end.

No.

It was only the beginning . . .

THE LAST WORD:

THE SACRED FAMILY

"There are a lot more going on, that people realize," Kathy said one day.

"What do you mean?" I asked.

"Every second counts, Meckron. Every thought, every doing."

"I . . . Are you talking about the fate of the Mankind?"

"Yes."

"What is the fate of the Mankind, Kathy?"

"The fate of the Mankind is to become The Sacred Family. The question when it will happen, is up to you guys, down there."

According to the Angel Realms, it goes like this:

The people of a different races have lived on the Earth for billions of years.

By fulfilling the dream of the Creator, that Human Being will be like Him one day, can powerfully illuminate the Allness like He can, a wonderful jorney have been arranged through the Eras for the Child of the God.

But the each Era only bears some major Soul Wisdoms.

In the course of a human history, there has been a lot of these epochs.

One of them lasts about 100 000 years plus 9000 years of transition. These Eras were in a form of a triple—The Era of the Vedism (where the Mankind lived closest to the God, communicating with Him and His realness was clear to everyone as it is clear for the angels), The Era of the Visualization (in which the human race developed Live Images and shapes of an ideas in their mind, creating a new visions of existence) and The Era of the Occult (where they began to worship the images and the visions of the illusions).

But so far, all of these circles of the Ages led to a global catastrophe.

This disaster embodies the important goal, which was organized as a transition of the Mankind to lead them to their new "lessons" and the old "study materials" were wiped out from the planet Earth, buried deep down in the ground to the planet`s core for purification.

But this time . . .

It is the first time in the history of mankind, where it`s going to be different.

A new dawn is coming, a new era.

The Era of the likes of which have never been seen.

The Era in which we repair our own past, clean up the garbage and scrubbing ourselves clean in our Spirit, and then we don`t need the cleaning process—the "end of the world"!

Finally, there is a new hope in the Universe—the Mankind is finally ready for it!

The efforts of all the Angels and the Forces of Light bear fruit!

We live in a period, in which will expire Mayan and Aztec calendars, and the cosmic inplacement, the likes of which has not been for the past 26 000 years.

Even the Mayans and the Aztecs was not able to predict the next step for the Mankind.

But our Father, The God, our beloved Dad, have accelerated His energies again!

He believes again!

He hopes!

He dreams that His Child—The Human Being—eventually returns to Home, takes the place beside his Father, in creating the Light for the Universe, as our Dad dreamed for us!

And he hastened all the Energies of Infinity, accelerating them just like during the Creation of A Man, because in Him, has blossomed an inspiration and faith in His Child's next step.

Perhaps the most important step throughout the course of the Human History.

And we, the people, stand on the threshold of the Universal Current, which brings us an unparalleled opportunity to receive the Divine Inspiration.

21.12.2012 reflects the increased cooperation between the three planets—Neptune (which represents the higher spirituality), Pluto (representing transfiguration) and Uranium (representing the change of our counciousness).

It seems as the language of the Universe is trying to tell us what steps our Dad expects from us.

Such planets` cooperation helps to make a major changes for the planet Earth's inhabitants` shared counciosness.

Of course, such energetic time can also be used unwisely.

That is why I call all the people to heal their emotions and thoughts and energies.

Body, soul and spirit.

So that we could use this very important moment for the benefit of the Universe—for the sole purpose, which the Allness awaits and hopes from the Mankind!

Oh, how much joy and light could it bring to ourselves and to everyone and to our Dad!

As a sign of the arrival of an important Era, there are many facts around us.

The Higher Angels are present, the wise old souls incarnating, the Indigo Children, the Crystal Children, etc.

That's why the Earth's population is now so big!

This means that our Dad collects the best souls, heroes and the lightworkers, from all over the history of Mankind, to support and prepare the world for our next step.

Also, for many of the people, it has become easy to channel the Angels and the Lightbeings.

And the mental changes are taking place in everyone`s life with an enormous speed.

Also, in the energetic world, it is seen as the Dark Forces panic, hasting in desperation, because of the Era of the Harmony that is coming.

So, how can we use these changes for the Higher Good?

The secret is in you!

In every one of you—in every Child of a God—please identify the Truth with your own feelings, bring the harmony and the balance in your lives, cheering in a lightful peace, and then we can perceive a New World.

We can percieve what our Dad expects from us. What do we expect from ourselves.

We can feel, we can dream of what could be real in the New World?

What the World should be like, for our highly spiritual children?

We have an opportunity to change the Earth, as it was in The Beginning, in the Paradise.

But this can not be done, until the human race realizes the destructiveness of the technocratic world and the exxageration of our ways.

That so-called "civilized society" is based on a dividing in pieces the perfect links of the Creation of our Father, dwelling more far and far from the Whole Meaning, the Truth.

After all, our Dad loves us forever.

He gave us everything.

If He would have thought that we would be better off, if He gave us all the Creation in pieces, in tiny particles, which no longer has the cooperation with each other and lost the Whole Meaning, then He would have done so.

So we definately need to come to an understanding, that to create a new, there is no need to destroy the old.

And such an understanding would stop us to destroy our planet Earth.

This is the first step to prevent a global catastrophe. In order to move into a New Era, without the indispensable "cleaning program".

But our Dad always hopes, believes! Eternally.

Believes, that the Mankind will look at the beautiful dawn, suddenly seeing Him and themselves and the creation, in all it`s beauty and harmony, which He created so perfect for us.

To see and understand the definition of the all!

To live forever, in His gift of an earthly paradise where everything is all there, where people can create the Light without a worry!

But I see the beautiful gardens with our Dad, in my vision!

I see the happy people.

Look! I`ll show you the pictures from the future, my dears.

Look!

A little child is playing with a bee, do you see? The bee doesn`t sting him, because the boy carries the purity of the divinity, such as it is in the nature of the God.

And the child smiles to the sun, to a blue sky, thinking:

"What a wonderful life my fathers and mothers gave me, they kept a paradise for me!

How good it is that they kept all that loves me! And I love in return!"

And this high-spiritually advanced child of God lives forever, and reincarnating in the nature, which the wise ancestors of his had kept for him, when the world heard the first notes of a New Era.

His parents cleaned all the dirt, which could stain the Human Soul, the mind and the body.

And you can see how clean everything is?

The beautiful ancient Living Engrained Homes of our ancestors, ringing in the atmosphere of Love and giving wonderful aromas of the blooming all around.

The homes and the gardens, a little Paradises, which represent the original garden of the Dad, when He first created a home for His children. The ancestral Living Engrained Homes, blossoming as the little Universes, honoring the time when God created the Garden of Eden, for the birth of a Man.

And all will live in harmony with everything.

If there is no dirt, there can only be the harmony.

They live in happy lives, because they returned back from the brink of a chaos.

And they cleaned away all that was dirty and toxic, and was born in the previous eras, from the destructive thoughts.

From the Dark Forces.

And no evil could ever touch anyone, as the Divine Wisdom from the previous Eras—the Lines of Times—and from the Soul and from our Dad, lived in them, as it lived in the people who walked the Earth in previous eras, Creating side-by-side with our Dad.

And our Dad can be close to everyone.

Every little grass, a spring water, a healing and vital roots—they all speak of His endless love for us.

About His love for the people, for his wise Sons and Daughters!

And about the Child, who loves his Father and about a Home!

About His love for a happy child who lives in the Atmosphere of Love and who keeps it and shares it with the others!

And so the Light of God—the Blessing Bluish Light—only increases in every moment, mirroring from the Father`s and His Child`s love!

Once again, our omnipresent Father, our beloved Dad, could shine brighter than the Sun, in the middle of the sky, both day and night, over the Universe, emitting His special Light of His Soul.

Again, all the existing and percieving and thinking energies and beings of the Universe, can recognize our Creator and the Creation as a perfect one, a good and wise.

The Allness will see the Blessing Bluish Light, that planet Earth is emitting, when the Human Beings have fulfilled their every moment with that Light.

Just like our Dad does.

And our dear Dad feels His Child's warmth of love, the light of his wisdom and goodness of the soul.

And also the Energy of Love—the soulmate of the God—who has descended on the planet Earth, also sees that the Mankind himself is able to emit the same amount of the Light of Love, that she could.

So the Energy of Love can finally return to her lover, to her soulmate. To our Dad.

Not as a particle, but as in full Light.

And through her gentle illumination, our Dad will once again reappear, being visible in all dimensions.

Sensing, thinking, dreaming and creating like our Dad, through the eternity of billions of years, we may finally be as a family again.

The Sacred Family—the God as a Father, the Energy of Love as a Mother and a Human Being—a their beloved Child.

This Sacred Family will live in the Creation, the Harmony and the Light, bringing joy and blessings to everything and everyone through the co-creation.

My dear dear dad—the Creator! My dear mom—the Energy of Love! My dear brothers and sisters—the People!

We will be happy again!

Together!

All this, my dears, can offer us our next step!

Only, please, imagine!

Dream!

What would you like your next step, born in the Light, to be?

What would it be, to be worthy of our Dad? Worthy of all the people to come, our children?

Worthy of ourselves, our own soul?

What would you like to inherit to everyone in the Eternity?